MARGARET
THATCHER
OF GREAT BRITAIN

IN FOCUS BIOGRAPHIES

ROBERT MUGABE OF ZIMBABWE
BY RICHARD WORTH

MARGARET THATCHER OF GREAT BRITAIN
BY MARIETTA D. MOSKIN

IN FOCUS

MARGARET THATCHER
OF GREAT BRITAIN

M A R I E T T A   D.   M O S K I N

JULIAN MESSNER

Copyright © 1990 by Marietta D. Moskin
All rights reserved including the right of
reproduction in whole or in part in any form.
Published by Julian Messner, a division of
Silver Burdett Press, Inc., Simon & Schuster, Inc.
Prentice Hall Bldg., Englewood Cliffs, NJ 07632

JULIAN MESSNER and colophon are trademarks of
Simon & Schuster, Inc. Design by Leslie Bauman.
Manufactured in the United States of America.

Lib. ed.   10 9 8 7 6 5 4 3 2 1
Paper ed.   10 9 8 7 6 5 4 3 2 1

Library of Congress Cataloging-in-Publication Data

Moskin, Marietta D.
Margaret Thatcher of Great Britain/Marietta D. Moskin.
p.   cm.—(In focus biographies)
Includes bibliographical references.
Summary: Follows the life and political career of Great Britain's
first female prime minister.
1. Thatcher, Margaret—Juvenile literature.   2. Prime ministers—
Great Britain Biography—Juvenile literature. [1. Thatcher,
Margaret.   2. Prime ministers.]   I. Title.   II. Series.
DA591.T47M67   1990
941.085′8′092dc20
[B]
[92]   ISBN 0-671-69633-5 paper   90-31582
ISBN 0-671-69632-7 LSB   CIP
AC

CONTENTS

PREFACE

A street scene in London, England: a crowd of onlookers at a public building stands gaping as a sleek black limousine rolls up, carefully guarded by helmeted bobbies, as London policemen are called. The well-groomed, beautifully gowned and jeweled woman who emerges from the car smiles graciously and waves to the eager crowd.

The queen of England? No. The woman in the black Daimler is in a political sense much more powerful than Queen Elizabeth II. She is Margaret Hilda Thatcher, who has served as prime minister of Great Britain since the queen ceremonially appointed her to that office in 1979. While the queen, as head of state, serves her people mostly in a ceremonial capacity, it is Margaret Thatcher, the prime minister, who sits with other world leaders at conference tables and shapes the political and economic realities of British life.

British prime ministers, unlike American presidents, are not elected directly by the people. When one of Britain's two major political parties wins a majority of seats in Parliament during a general election, the leader of that party is appointed prime minister by the monarch. The party leader is chosen from among and by party members who hold seats in Parliament, England's lawmaking body. More precisely, the prime minister emerges from the House of Commons, the lower of the two houses of Parliament. Members of Parliament (MPs) are elected by the general public. Members of the upper house of Parliament, the House of Lords, are not elected. They include important bishops and archbishops, the lords spiritual, and most members of Britain's peerage, known as the lords temporal. These peers have a hereditary right to a seat in the House of Lords. Other peers are appointed for life by the monarch in recognition of distinguished service to the nation. They cannot pass on their seats to their heirs. The power of the House of Lords to effect legislation is very limited.

In 1975 Margaret Thatcher became the first woman in British history to attain the position of leader of her party. Her party is the staid Conservative (or Tory) party whose members heavily represent the traditional moneyed and landowning sections of British society. Her predecessors include such famous men as the duke of Wellington, Benjamin Disraeli, Sir Winston Churchill, Sir Anthony Eden, and Sir Alec Douglas-Home. Like some of these predecessors Margaret Thatcher came to office without the benefits of an illustrious aristocratic ancestry. Her rise in the Conservative party was the result of her own abilities and hard work. When the Tories won an electoral victory over the ruling Labour party in 1979, their leader, Margaret Thatcher, automatically became the prime minister of England.

By 1989 Margaret Thatcher had been in office longer than any previous British prime minister in the twentieth century. In terms of service, she is also the senior participant in international gatherings of major world leaders. When Margaret Thatcher speaks, the world listens, even if many of those listeners do not always agree with her.

How did the daughter of a small-town grocer rise to such a position of power and responsibility? This book will trace the influences that shaped Margaret Thatcher's social, political, and economic ideas. It will examine her approach to life, and explain how she reached the pinnacle of British politics. You will see how Margaret Thatcher differs from other prime ministers and how, or whether, she has changed this historic institution. And you will learn about her triumphs and failures as she continues to implement her own dreams for England's future.

1

NUMBER 10 DOWNING STREET

I n the United States, when we think of the hub of governmental power, the White House comes to mind. But what is the equivalent center of power in England? One is tempted to think of Buckingham Palace, the sprawling London residence of the queen. But in fact, Buckingham Palace is not the equivalent of our White House. The center of governmental power in Britain is an unassuming narrow gray house, one of a row of attached buildings tucked away in a small side street in the Whitehall section of London. Only the uniformed bobbies guarding the house around the clock and the constant presence of curious sightseers are clues that something important must be going on inside. The address is Number 10 Downing Street, the official residence of Britain's prime minister.

N

SCOTLAND

ATLANTIC
OCEAN

GREAT BRITAIN

Edinburgh

NORTHERN
IRELAND
Belfast

NORTH SEA

IRISH SEA

THE
MIDLANDS

Dublin

Nottingham

REPUBLIC
OF
IRELAND

Grantham

ENGLAND

WALES
Cardiff

Oxford

Thames
River

London

Dartford

BEL

Brighton

FRANC

miles 100

ENGLISH CHANNEL

kilometers 150

Forty-eight British prime ministers have inhabited the Downing Street building since 1735. Some of them have lived in the house more than once. It was a memorable occasion when, on May 4, 1979, the newest of Britain's prime ministers walked through the distinctive black door with its iron lion-head knocker. For the first time, a woman was taking up residence at Downing Street, not as a wife or daughter, but as the main tenant!

By entering Number 10 Downing Street, Margaret Thatcher made history for the second time on that fourth day of May. Scarcely more than two hours earlier she had been summoned to Buckingham Palace for the traditional "hand-kissing" ceremony during which Queen Elizabeth II asked her to form a new government. As the head of the political party that had just won a landslide victory at the British polls, Margaret Thatcher was given the linked titles of prime minister and first lord of the Treasury. Queen Elizabeth had performed the ceremony six times since she ascended to the throne in 1952. But this was the first time that she, or any British monarch for that matter, had bestowed the titles on a woman.

For Margaret Thatcher the "hand-kissing" ceremony was the climax of a lifelong effort to reach the top in her profession. The road to the top in politics is difficult for anyone. For a woman it is even more difficult. Just a few years earlier Margaret Thatcher, MP and cabinet minister, could hardly have hoped to achieve the top political spot in the country.

Now, as she crossed the black and white marble-tiled entrance hall of her new residence and climbed the stairs past the portraits of her distinguished predecessors, her joy certainly must have been tempered by the knowledge that she had just stepped into one of the world's most difficult and most responsible jobs.

Although the British monarch is still thought of as the head of state, the present-day British prime minister, or PM, serves in every sense as the head of government. The PM has the power to appoint and dismiss cabinet ministers, to preside over cabinet meetings, and to have the final say when governmental policies and priorities are set. When a policy is challenged, the prime minister can ask the queen to dissolve Parliament and call for new elections if such a move seems politically wise. For their part, leaders of the party out of power—the Opposition—can force the prime minister to ask for new elections through a parliamentary vote of "no confidence."

An older and somewhat secondary function is the prime minister's role as intermediary between Parliament and the queen. It is the prime minister who informs the queen of cabinet decisions and about bills introduced before Parliament. The queen must give her consent to all bills passed although, by custom, she never ignores her minister's advice. Prime ministers, in turn, can continue in office only as long as they command majority support and loyalty in Parliament.

EARLIER PRIME MINISTERS

In June 1979, at the beginning of her first term in office, Mrs. Thatcher might have envied some of her earliest predecessors, who dealt with a much less complicated government. True, earlier prime ministers had less power, as English monarchs still made many important decisions. Over the centuries, however, royal powers were gradually curtailed. At the Council of Runnymede in 1215, for example, feudal lords obtained certain rights under a written royal charter now known as the Magna Carta. In the centuries that followed, nobles were gradually joined by representatives of the common people in more formal assemblies called Parliaments. The commoners now had an opportunity to present grievances and petitions to the monarch. By 1689 the commoners in Parliament had grown strong enough to impose their collective will not only on the Crown but on their noble counterparts in the House of Lords. A Bill of Rights granted Parliament special rights to control taxes and legislation, with financial powers particularly ceded to the House of Commons. Without control over the purse strings, monarchs had far fewer opportunities to abuse their other powers.

By the early 1700s, England's system of government had become much more complicated than it had been in the days of Runnymede. The monarch was surrounded by too many counselors (ministers), and the Privy Council—a select body of personal advisers—had become too unwieldy. For practical purposes the monarch began to rely on a small group of ministers to help him or her make decisions and to persuade Parliament to translate these decisions into law. Because these special ministers met in a small room called a cabinet, they eventually became known as the monarch's cabinet.

In 1714 a German prince assumed the British throne as King George I. George spoke little English and knew even less about England. He left much of the day-to-day governing to his cabinet. He relied particularly on his first lord of the Treasury, Sir Robert Walpole. His jealous colleagues referred to Walpole as the "prime" minister because of his special influence on the king. Walpole disclaimed his "primacy," but the mocking title stuck. Each succeeding cabinet was headed by a prime minister who ranked above his peers. The title prime minister did not become official, however, until 1905.

Under King George III—he was the one who lost the American colonies—even more power trickled down from the Crown to the cabinet. George III was certainly the most hated man of his time in the American colonies. But he created many problems for his English subjects, too. As he sank deeper and deeper into mental illness, his prime minister, William Pitt the Younger, had to assume more and more responsibility to keep the government functioning. While succeeding monarchs up through Queen Victoria still were active rulers, their powers were eroded. Today, for all practical purposes, British monarchs reign while their prime ministers "run the store."

BRITISH PRIME MINISTERS AND THEIR PARTIES

Sir Robert Walpole	1721–1742	Whig
Spencer Compton	1742–1743	Whig
Henry Pelham	1743–1754	Whig
Duke of Newcastle	1754–1756	Whig
Duke of Devonshire	1756–1757	Whig
Duke of Newcastle (2)	1757–1762	Whig
Earl of Bute	1762–1763	Tory
George Grenville	1763–1765	Whig
Marquis of Rockingham	1765–1766	Whig
William Pitt (Elder)	1766–1768	Whig
Duke of Grafton	1768–1770	Whig
Lord North	1770–1782	Tory
Marquis of Rockingham (2)	1782–1783	Whig
Duke of Portland	1783	Tory
William Pitt (Younger)	1783–1801	Tory
Henry Addington	1801–1804	Tory
William Pitt (Younger)(2)	1804–1806	Tory
Lord Grenville	1806–1807	Whig
William Bentinck, Duke of Portland	1807–1809	Tory
Spencer Perceval	1809–1812	Tory
Duke of Portland (2)	1807–1809	Tory
Earl of Liverpool	1812–1827	Tory
George Canning	1827	Tory
Lord Goderich	1827–1828	Tory
Duke of Wellington	1828–1830	Tory
Earl Grey	1830–1834	Whig
Lord Melbourne	1834	Whig
Sir Robert Peel	1834–1835	Tory
Lord Melbourne (2)	1835–1841	Whig
Sir Robert Peel (2)	1841–1846	Tory

Lord John Russell	1846–1852	Whig
Earl of Derby	1852	Conservative
Earl of Aberdeen	1852–1855	Coalition
Viscount Palmerston	1855–1858	Liberal
Earl of Derby (2)	1858–1859	Conservative
Viscount Palmerston (2)	1859–1865	Liberal
Lord John Russell (2)	1865–1866	Whig
Earl of Derby (3)	1866–1868	Conservative
Benjamin Disraeli	1868	Conservative
William E. Gladstone	1868–1874	Liberal
Benjamin Disraeli (2)	1874–1880	Conservative
William E. Gladstone (2)	1880–1885	Liberal
Marquis of Salisbury	1885–1886	Conservative
William E. Gladstone (3)	1886	Liberal
Marquis of Salisbury (2)	1886–1892	Conservative
William E. Gladstone (4)	1892–1894	Liberal
Earl of Rosebery	1894–1895	Liberal
Marquis of Salisbury (3)	1895–1902	Conservative
Arthur James Balfour	1902–1905	Conservative
Sir Henry Campbell-Bannerman	1905–1908	Liberal
Herbert Henry Asquith	1908–1916	Liberal
David Lloyd George	1916–1922	Coalition
Andrew Bonar Law	1922–1923	Conservative
Stanley Baldwin	1923–1924	Conservative
James Ramsay MacDonald	1924	Labour
Stanley Baldwin (2)	1924–1929	Conservative
James Ramsay MacDonald (2)	1929–1935	Labour
Stanley Baldwin (3)	1935–1937	Conservative
Neville Chamberlain	1937–1940	National
Sir Winston Churchill	1940–1945	Coalition
Clement Attlee	1945–1951	Labour
Sir Winston Churchill (2)	1951–1955	Conservative
Sir Anthony Eden	1955–1957	Conservative
Harold Macmillan	1957–1963	Conservative

Sir Alec Douglas-Home	1963–1964	Conservative
Harold Wilson	1964–1970	Labour
Edward Heath	1970–1974	Conservative
Harold Wilson (2)	1974–1976	Labour
James Callaghan	1976–1979	Labour
Margaret Hilda Thatcher	1979	Conservative

Source: *Number 10: The Private Lives of Six Prime Ministers*
by Terence Feely, London: Sidgwick & Jackson, 1982.

The "store" in this case is the modest-looking house in Downing Street. Because Margaret Thatcher was born above her father's grocery store, people like to joke that she has come full circle because she now "lives above the store" again. Officially, laws are made in the huge ornate Parliament buildings that stretch out for several blocks along the nearby Thames River. But the nerve center of the British government is the cabinet room at 10 Downing Street. The house was given to Sir Robert Walpole in 1735 by King George II to serve as the prime minister's office and residence. Except for a few structural changes to the facade in 1772, the house remains almost exactly the way it was in Sir Robert Walpole's days.

Mrs. Thatcher's private quarters at Downing Street are in the "attic" above the state rooms. Many earlier prime ministers found the private apartment cramped in contrast to their own large homes and decided not to live there. The Thatchers, who moved to Downing Street from a small house in a fashionable section of London called Chelsea, like it just fine.

The Downing Street house takes its name from the man who built the row of houses in 1680. Sir George Downing served his country alternately as a foreign envoy and a spy, and was granted the land on Downing Street as a reward for his efforts. In time the houses reverted to the Crown.

Number 10 Downing Street isn't as small as it looks from the outside. Before the residence was offered to Walpole, it had been

May 4, 1979. Margaret Thatcher and her husband Denis wave to well-wishers as they enter Number 10 Downing Street. Mrs. Thatcher is the first woman to serve as prime minister of Great Britain.

greatly enlarged to include a substantial house and garden in the back and one of the two adjacent houses. The house was offered to Walpole as a personal gift, but the prime minister accepted it on behalf of future first lords of the Treasury in perpetuity. The brass letter box at the door of the house still bears the legend "First Lord of the Treasury."

As a result of Walpole's action, the cost of any repairs to the building is assumed by the British government. However, all other expenses of running the house, including the wages of the domestic staff and the cost of entertaining, are carried by the incumbent prime minister. In return, prime ministers get to live at Downing Street rent-free. Until 1937, free housing was their only financial reward for taking on the burdens of the office. Those earlier prime ministers surely needed to have private incomes to afford the honor.

In her rent-free home Margaret Thatcher oversees the upkeep of more than sixty rooms. Many of these rooms are used as offices for Mrs. Thatcher and her various assistants. The large state rooms are used to entertain royal visitors and foreign dignitaries. Prime ministers and their families are free to use any of the official rooms at Downing Street as they please. However, they may not make any structural changes without special permission. Redecorating often has to be at the prime minister's own expense. But the PM can and does borrow furniture and paintings from various museums in order to change the looks of the state rooms.

Prime ministers bring their own furnishings to decorate their private quarters. This causes something of an upheaval when governments change after an election. American presidents have almost two months between administrations during which the outgoing first family can pack and the incoming one can make arrangements at leisure. In England, the transition from one government to the next is instantaneous and can come with little notice when special elections are called. Quick transitions are possible because the political party out of power maintains a full "shadow cabinet," which becomes fully operational the moment an election is won.

On June 4, 1979, as Margaret Thatcher and her husband Denis waited for the call from Buckingham Palace and while they attended the forty-five minute installation ceremony, feverish activity went on at Downing Street. The family of the outgoing prime minister, James Callaghan, was preparing to vacate the premises even as flowers for the new prime minister began to arrive.

Number 10 Downing Street has an efficient household staff. By the time Mrs. Thatcher was ushered into her new home, it is almost certain that no evidence of the previous occupants could be observed.

2

THE GROWING-UP YEARS

G rantham, Lincolnshire, sits in the center of the Midlands, a long, narrow, and largely industrial area that stretches northward through England's midsection. The villages and towns of the Midlands are not as beautiful as the old villages of southeast England, the Cotswolds, or Wales. Nottingham, the big town nearest to Grantham, stretches for miles in a mixed sprawl of factories, mine entrances, and slag heaps. Agriculture is still a major occupation nearer to Grantham which serves farmers as a market town. It has also long been a center of locomotive and diesel manufacturing.

In past centuries Grantham was an important stopping place for stagecoaches along England's great Northern Road. Like almost every town and village in the British Isles, it has its share of historical memories. Guidebooks boast that the town's venerable old inn, the Angel and Royal, was used by the Knights Templar during the Crusades. King John held court there in 1213, and King Richard III stopped at the Angel and Royal in 1483. Sir Isaac Newton went to school in Grantham. He was the famous mathematician who discovered the role of gravity in holding together the universe after seeing an apple fall from a tree. Charles Dickens wrote his novel *Nicholas Nickleby* while staying in another famous local inn, the George.

Someday the guidebooks will surely report that Grantham is also the birthplace of Prime Minister Margaret Thatcher, who was born above her father's grocery store at the corner of North Parade and Broad streets on October 13, 1925.

Much has been made of Margaret Thatcher's humble beginnings and of the fact that the apartment above the store had neither running hot water nor an indoor bathroom. Future generations of English schoolchildren will probably learn about these hardships the way American students read about Abraham Lincoln's humble log cabin home. But legends can be deceptive. Margaret Thatcher and her older sister, Muriel, certainly didn't regard themselves as poor or deprived as they grew up in Grantham during the 1920s and 1930s.

Alfred Roberts, Margaret's father, had come to Grantham while still in his teens to manage a small grocery store. Storekeeping was not the family trade. Alfred came from a long line of boot makers, but his poor eyesight made it impossible for him to follow that trade. Apprenticed to a grocer after leaving school at age thirteen, young Alfred did well enough to rise to management level before he was twenty. To make up for his lack of education, he became a voracious reader, borrowing biographies and books on politics from local libraries. He did his self-imposed homework well. Later in life Alfred became a well-informed speaker, a Methodist lay preacher, and served on the board of a local school.

The grocery store formerly owned by Alfred and Beatrice Roberts, Margaret's parents, as it looked in 1979. The Roberts family lived in an apartment above the store.

In Grantham, Alfred joined the Methodist church where he met his future wife, Beatrice Stephenson, a skilled seamstress. They worked hard and saved enough money to buy a grocery store of their own at the edge of town. The store, with the family apartment above, was in a fairly large building. It eventually housed various food departments as well as a small post office and a tobacco shop. Alfred Roberts ran a tight ship. Although he could gradually afford to hire helpers—up to eight in later years—either he or Beatrice remained in the store to supervise operations. As a result, the Roberts family rarely spent time together outside of their store. Alfred's strict Methodist beliefs did not permit any frivolities on Sunday, the family's one day off. All of them attended services four times on that day. Alfred campaigned hard to keep the town's only movie theater closed on Sundays, and his children were not permitted to play with their toys on that day.

All of this meant that Muriel and Margaret spent a great deal of time in the store while they were growing up. For Margaret it was an apprenticeship of sorts, although she could not have known it at the time. Her father, whom Margaret admired and adored, became more and more interested in local politics. Small-town general stores are often meeting places where neighborhood people gather to exchange news and gossip. For an aspiring politician a store is an excellent place to gather support and express opinions to many willing listeners.

Alfred Roberts climbed the local political ladder and became borough councillor, then alderman, and finally mayor of Grantham. His shop became a meeting place for those who shared his political ideas and his dreams. At election time the store became the place where campaign pamphlets were sorted, folded, and addressed. After school, Muriel and Margaret were drafted to help. They also worked in the store, slicing cheese and meat, weighing butter, selling candies and cakes, scooping rice and beans out of the big barrels and bags in which such staples were then still delivered to stores. While their hands were busy, the two sisters absorbed the political talk. Over the years Alfred Roberts's conservative, frugal, and stern moral and religious ideas were deeply imprinted on his younger daughter.

LIFE IN GRANTHAM

The 1920s and early 1930s were hard times in England, as they were all over the world. The upheaval of World War I had shattered many old traditions and conventions. Soldiers returning from the battlefields of Europe had greater ambitions and expectations for their future lives. However, their dreams were hampered by poor economic conditions and widespread unemployment. And although the rigid divisions of the British class system were changing, people still generally knew and kept "their place" in the social pyramid. The aristocracy and the landed gentry were on top of the social pyramid. They had special privileges. At the bottom were farm laborers and factory workers who owned neither property nor land. In between were the professionals: lawyers, doctors, clergy, and people "in trade"—a term that could apply to the owners of the largest factory as well as to the proprietor of the corner grocery store. A large amount of money could blur some of these class distinctions and many wealthy businessmen managed to buy their way into society. Still, class prejudices lingered.

The Roberts family might have been considered poor by present-day, middle-class standards. But when Margaret was growing up, she was certainly aware that she and her family were better off than most of the people in her immediate neighborhood. The Robertses lived literally on the edge of Grantham's "right side of the tracks." The railroad tracks and a public housing project could be seen from the back windows of their home while well-kept town houses lined the other side of their street. Alfred Roberts certainly identified himself more with the propertied people in the town than with the laborers and factory workers living in the council estates, or public housing projects, nearby.

Grantham did not suffer as much from the Great Depression of the early 1930s as other parts of England did, but there was unemployment and there were hungry people waiting in breadlines. And as Margaret grew older, there were also the distant rumblings of an approaching war. Continental Europe, across the narrow English Channel, was in turmoil. Civil war was raging in Spain and fascism was on the rise in Germany and Italy. For Margaret Roberts, however, the major concern in those years was school.

Although there was an elementary school only a couple of blocks away from the Roberts home, Alfred did not consider it good enough for his daughters. Muriel and Margaret attended a school more than a mile away in a better middle-class neighborhood.

Former teachers and classmates remember Margaret Roberts as a pretty, round-faced, blue-eyed little girl, a little too serious for her age. Her sister Muriel is remembered as friendly, popular, and outgoing, but many felt that Margaret had no sense of humor and that she did little to make friends. Others felt she was too goody-goody, the kind of child held up to them as an example by parents and teachers: "Why can't you be as good as Margaret Roberts?"

On the other hand, Margaret was never shy. She knew her worth at an early age. She asked questions in class and debated with teachers. When she was nine she won a poetry-reading contest at a town fair. "You are a lucky girl, Margaret," a teacher told her, meaning to praise. Margaret looked her teacher straight in the eyes. "It wasn't luck. I deserved it," she said. And she has felt like that about her many successes in life ever since.

At eleven, Margaret sat for the dreaded "eleven-plus" exam. Until just a few years ago, this exam hung like a shadow over the lives of most English schoolchildren. It was designed to separate gifted from average students. Those who passed had the opportunity to advance into a college preparatory grammar school. Others went on to ordinary schools with few options after graduation. Some went on to vocational schools, others to work at fifteen or sixteen.

The testing was terribly unfair. Many children are not ready at age eleven to demonstrate their full potential for further learning. If a child who needed free public education failed the exam, the path to future higher education and better job opportunities was virtually cut off. This was not true for the well-to-do. Their parents could afford to hire tutors. They could be sent to independent elementary schools and later to private preparatory schools (known as "public schools" in England), which were designed to help students pass the rigorous entrance exams to Oxford and Cambridge, England's most prestigious centers of higher learning. There are many fine regional colleges and universities in England. The majority of graduates of the government-funded grammar

Grantham Grammar School. Margaret Roberts is sitting in the front row, fifth from the right.

schools usually find places in these other universities. But each year some very bright grammar school students are accepted at Oxford or Cambridge.

Margaret Roberts reached the first rung on her ladder to success when she passed the eleven-plus exam and was accepted at the Grantham and Estevan Girls' Grammar School. Of course, neither she nor her family expected her to fail.

Margaret was not considered brilliant at Grantham School, but she was consistently one of the top students in her class by dint of effort and hard work. As at the lower school, her classmates considered her somewhat boring and stand-offish. Part of the problem was her family's strict standards. For example, Margaret and Muriel were not permitted to attend the dances and parties that were a normal part of school life. Margaret took piano lessons and participated in sports, but the rest of her free time was devoted to helping at home, working in the store, and assisting Alf Roberts in his political activities. From age ten she exhibited skill in bringing reluctant and unmotivated voters to the polling place on election day. At an even earlier age Margaret attended political meetings for her father and reported to him what had gone on. To young Margaret Roberts, political activism was a normal part of growing up, just like going to school and playing field hockey.

From their plain, quiet mother the two Roberts girls learned various housekeeping skills, including careful money management, cooking, painting, and wallpapering. Margaret learned to make her own clothes, to shop prudently, and to make do with what she could afford. Luxuries, such as a bicycle, had to be saved for or earned. The Roberts family emphasized the values of duty, hard work, initiative, self-reliance, and self-denial.

The few times when Margaret complained that she could not do the things her friends were doing, her father was ready with his answer.

"Never do things or want to do things just because other people do them," he told her. "Make up your mind about what you are going to do and persuade people to go your way."

There was enormous stress on the value of work. Again and again Alf Roberts taught his girls that work was important and idleness a waste. In his view, life had to be used for some good purpose to be lived to the full.

Margaret learned self-control. She also learned to avoid self-pity, to accept her failures silently, and then to try again, if necessary, in a different way. In later life Margaret remembered the advice of her first headmistress, Miss Williams: "You must not be too satisfied with what you have done. You must try to do better. Whatever you have, you must try to live up to the best that is within you."

From her grandmother, who lived with the Roberts family for some years, Margaret learned that if a thing was worth doing, it was worth doing well. Grandmother Roberts was full of little sayings such as "Waste not, want not," and "Cleanliness is next to godliness."

THE WAR YEARS

In the late 1930s, while Margaret was growing up, Europe was moving closer to war. Even in Grantham, the people heard echoes of what was happening across the English Channel. Germany was flexing its muscles and menacing its neighbors. In 1938, the Nazi leader Adolf Hitler annexed parts of Czechoslovakia and all of Austria. Margaret's older sister Muriel was corresponding with a pen pal in Austria, a young Jewish girl. The Roberts family was horrified to learn through her letters about the brutalities committed by the Nazis against the Jews in Austria. A plea for help from the girl's parents caused Alfred Roberts to bring his daughter's pen pal to Grantham. From their Austrian guest, the teenage Margaret learned much about the evils of anti-Semitism, fascism, and unbridled governmental powers. These memories affected her friendly attitude toward Israel in later years.

When World War II finally broke out in 1939, Margaret was in high school. Grantham's munitions factories drew heavy bombing during the war, and nights were punctuated by air-raid sirens. The effects of the war were felt by everyone in Grantham. Young men went off to the fighting. Shortages of goods were common. People had to use ration books and coupons to buy food and clothing. Meat was scarce, and families had to be registered with a butcher to get it at all. Choices were limited, and life revolved around the war. The wartime hardships affected Margaret deeply. Later, in her public life, she would often recall the lack of choices during World War II.

Food shortages were less noticeable for the Roberts family. Because they owned a grocery store, there was always food around. In fact, Alf Roberts's business prospered. His store was large, with fine mahogany shelves and fittings and an increasing number of clerks. It certainly was no hardship for Mr. Roberts to pay Margaret's £13 ($72) annual school fee, a requirement even in government-supported schools. If it hadn't been for wartime austerity, the Roberts family probably could have afforded indoor plumbing in the late 1930s.

Meanwhile, Margaret was dreaming of her future. Her sister Muriel, less academically inclined, was being trained for a career in physiotherapy. Margaret's aim was higher. There was never any doubt in her mind that she was university-bound. But now she was dreaming of Oxford. It was a big ambition for a small-town girl of modest means. Students from local grammar schools, and even those who attended the less exclusive private boarding schools, rarely aimed that high. Margaret's headmistress, Miss Gillies, tried to talk her out of it. There were special fees for students taking the exams for Oxford and Cambridge, and Grantham School was not prepared to pay these fees for Margaret. Even more serious, a prerequisite for entrance to Oxford was four years of Latin or the ability to pass a Latin exam.

Since Margaret had not studied Latin, this ought to have ended the matter right then and there. But Miss Gillies had not counted on her student's determination or on Alf Roberts's faith in his daughter's intelligence. He offered to pay for the Oxford exam and for the tutoring Margaret needed to prepare for the Latin exam.

Miss Gillies threw up her hands in the face of such determination. She herself would tutor Margaret in Latin with help from a Latin teacher at the nearby boys' high school. Margaret gave up her much-loved piano lessons and almost all other outside activities to concentrate on Latin. The hard work paid off. Within one year she managed to absorb four years of Latin, enough to do well on the exam. At age seventeen Margaret took and passed the entrance exam for Oxford. She was accepted and awarded a scholarship at

Somerville College, then one of only four women's colleges at Oxford University.

Margaret had to do one more thing to prepare for Oxford. In England, the way you speak is a clue to your status, class, and background. George Bernard Shaw exposed the snobbery of English class distinctions and speech patterns in his play *Pygmalion*, which was made into the musical and film *My Fair Lady*. Graduates of prestigious English schools like Eton and Harrow learned to speak the kind of clipped, clear English spoken by the British upper classes. Almost everyone else, including Margaret Roberts, had some kind of class or regional accent. Alfred Roberts was determined that his daughter would start at Oxford without any handicaps. Margaret Roberts was sent for elocution lessons.

In the fall of 1943, with war raging in Europe, Margaret Roberts left her hometown of Grantham, Lincolnshire, for the famous spired university city of Oxford. She went with her father's values and her grandmother's proverbs indelibly imprinted in her heart. She never forgot and took those rules and admonitions for her own. They guided her actions and convictions in her political life. In some ways the simple Grantham grocer who died in 1970 still inspires his daughter in her struggle to change the economic and political fabric of the England he loved.

3

FIRST STEPS IN POLITICS

The city of Oxford is a timeless place. In some ways it is two cities occupying the same space in different dimensions. There is the bustling modern town with its traffic-clogged High Street, surrounded by a residential area that soon yields to rolling green hills and farmlands—a "typical" English town. But within that busy, typical city center lies the other Oxford, the twelfth-century university town with its Gothic stone quadrangles, cloistered walkways, and ancient gray walls hiding well-kept gardens. There are thirty-five separate colleges in Oxford today. The oldest of these occupy large tracts in the very center of the town.

A walk through the narrow streets between endless stretches of massive stone wall transports one back to the Middle Ages, even as traffic roars past just a few blocks away.

At Oxford the townspeople and the college community exist side by side. Students and professors, sporting the black academic gowns they must still wear at many university functions, bicycle or walk among the shoppers and tourists on Carfax or Cornmarket Street.

When Margaret Roberts arrived in Oxford in 1943, the town was probably very much as it is today. There were more bicycles and fewer cars and buses in those days, however, because of wartime fuel shortages. There were also fewer students because so many young men had gone to war.

For the sheltered young woman from Grantham, Oxford was the beginning of a new and very different life. Margaret had rarely been away from home. While at home, she had lived within a very narrow circle. Suddenly she was mingling with the sons and daughters of nobility and with the brightest young people from the middle classes. Oxford has been the training ground for leaders in the British government and the foreign service for hundreds of years. Later, in Parliament, Margaret would find that many of her peers shared this university background with her. Some had actually been at Oxford when she was there, although few remembered her. Most prime ministers had been Oxford graduates. For someone hoping for a career in government service, an Oxford degree was almost indispensable.

Margaret's first problem was to decide on a field of study. She had given much thought to the subject before she left home. She was interested in the law, but this would entail years of study. Also, Margaret's financial circumstances would not make it practical. Her next impulse had been to train for a position in the Indian civil service. In the nineteenth century and in the first decades of the twentieth, large numbers of young people looked to Britain's overseas colonies for secure and profitable careers. In India, in Africa, and on Caribbean islands, there was a never-ending demand for British administrators and other officials to keep the empire running. Margaret had read Rudyard Kipling's romantic accounts of life in India. Miss Gillies, her headmistress from Grantham School, urged her to reconsider. She pointed out that the foreign civil service was very much a man's preserve. The competition would be fierce. Margaret argued that competing against men would make success even more creditable, but in the end, reality and common sense won out. At Somerville, a woman's college, she could excel in one of the sciences, where competition would be less than in history or literature. Miss Kay, a favorite science teacher, persuaded her to "read" chemistry at Oxford. Margaret respected this excellent teacher's advice. In addition, a knowledge of chemistry would permit her to earn a good living after graduation.

English universities are different from American colleges. Students work independently under the guidance of a special tutor whom they see weekly and who assigns readings or papers in their chosen subject. They do attend lectures and occasional seminars, but they spend much of their time in their college library and in one of the famous university libraries such as the Bodleian or the Radcliff Camera. That's why they are said to "read" whatever subject they have chosen.

Studying law was only a distant dream at this point, something to think about in the future. Margaret did reassure herself however, that a chemistry degree would not keep her from being accepted in law school. At this time she was not considering a political career. Economics was a factor. The pay for members of Parliament was much too low to permit someone without an outside income to make a living.

Oxford students study hard, but there are also many opportunities for recreation. On sunny afternoons, a popular pastime is punting flat boats along the Cherwell, a scenic river that flows through the city. There are gatherings at local pubs and tearooms, and students throw parties in their rooms. During the early 1940s, wartime needs required students to do volunteer work at various places. Margaret, like others, helped out in a canteen for soldiers.

The social atmosphere of Oxford was all very new and different for Margaret. At home, parties and drinking had been severely frowned upon. At Oxford, Margaret proved to be a skillful hostess, giving the expected sherry parties and making her guests mix and feel at ease, a useful skill for a future politician. She did not live at Somerville, but rented rooms in town, popularly known as "digs." Because her field of study required her to do many hours of laboratory work, Margaret had less free time than many other students. Despite this fact, she found the time to join the Oxford University Conservative Union. Originally, her reasons were purely social. The union was a place where she would meet many different people. It was also a rather natural move, given her long involvement with her father's political activities. Politics attracted Margaret, who loved debating and had proven her skill in high school. As a member of the Conservative Union she could sharpen her wits against many worthy opponents. Unfortunately, as a woman, she was barred from participating in the public debates presented at the famous Oxford Union Society. The society only started admitting women about twenty years ago, when some of the all-male Oxford colleges began to admit women. The Conservative Union did give Margaret a chance to do some public speaking and to canvass (solicit votes) door to door. She was chosen as the union's president in her last year at Oxford.

At Oxford, as at home, Margaret made few lasting friendships. She never had any real friendships with women. She did have a crush on a young lord, but the relationship had no chance of developing, given the social barriers of her time. Margaret never quite knew where she belonged. She did not belong with the social elite or with the bright middle-class girls who formed a clique of their own. When she spoke about home, she talked about her father, the mayor of Grantham, rather than Daddy the grocer. Some thought she talked about him too much.

The war in Europe ended in May 1945. Margaret was still at Oxford when the bells of the city and university rang out in joy. The elation brought by victory was short-lived, however. For England, the immediate postwar period was one of continued shortages, austerity, and political turmoil. To the dismay of many, England's wartime leader, Prime Minister Winston Churchill, was beaten by Labour leader Clement Attlee in the general elections of 1945. The man who had held England together and lifted British morale during the terrible war years had been rebuffed by the voters. Churchill's defeat seemed like a betrayal to Margaret. But the Labour party offered voters new proposals that many felt they could not resist.

The Labour party was something of an upstart among British political parties. It was not really fully organized until World War I (1914–1918). It did not win a majority in Parliament until 1924 and then for just a very brief period. There was a second Labour administration between 1929 and 1935. Before then, Conservatives and Liberals had alternated in forming governments and serving as the Opposition. They in turn had been the successors to the eighteenth-century Tories and Whigs. In 1945, however, Clement Attlee's program differed even from that of the previous Labour leader, Ramsay MacDonald. Attlee envisioned broad programs of social security, unemployment insurance, job security, government ownership of certain industries, and a great deal of central control over price and wages. His program appealed to many working people, but Conservatives saw it as a giant leap into socialism or, even worse, communism. In England this new, developing system became known as the welfare state.

Labour's emphasis on social welfare and union power seemed like heresy to Margaret Roberts. After all, she had grown up with her father's ideas about self-reliance and individual responsibility. Alf Roberts had started his political life as an Independent. He later became a liberal. By the beginning of World War II, Alf was a confirmed Conservative. Churchill's defeat in 1945 made Margaret an even more confirmed Conservative.

Margaret Roberts' first job was as a research chemist for a plastics company.

WORK AND MARRIAGE

Margaret graduated from Oxford in 1945 and immediately found a job as a research chemist with a plastics company in Manningtree, Essex, and moved to the nearby town of Colchester. Part of her job involved giving instructions to workers on the factory floor, the closest she ever came to direct involvement with laborers. For recreation she once again turned to politics. Margaret became an active volunteer in the local Conservative party organization, and she was soon noticed by party leaders. By now, even though her goal was still a law degree, a career in politics seemed a more possible ambition. Salaries for members of Parliament had been raised from £600 to £1,000 a year, about $5,600. In the late

1940s, that was enough money to enable someone without an outside income to manage. In 1949, Conservative party leaders recommended Margaret Roberts to the town of Dartford near London as a possible candidate for the upcoming election. After a series of interviews in which she competed with twenty men, Margaret was accepted as a candidate. She was only twenty-four years old, a fact that actually worked in her favor. As the youngest candidate for Parliament on record, and a female, she was given special attention by newspapers and other media. And with good reason. Voters saw a very young woman, barely out of school, who could speak fluently and without notes about complicated political and foreign-policy matters. Important people listened and took note.

The honor of her "adoption" as the Conservative candidate was somewhat hollow, however. Dartford was a safe Labour seat, and no Conservative candidate had won that seat for many years. Margaret did not expect to win the election, but it was a good learning opportunity. She had to go out canvassing, shaking hands with potential voters in her constituency, and giving speeches wherever she could. A constituency is comparable to an American congressional district. There is a separate one for every 60,000 voters in England. Some constituencies cover very small districts in heavily populated areas, while others in rural parts can stretch over many miles. Local party organizations select the candidate they would like to represent their district. Lists of likely candidates are drawn up, interviews are granted, and then a final selection is made. A constituency looks for a new candidate when an incumbent retires or dies—in which case there is a special by-election—or if a previous candidate has lost too many times and is nudged into withdrawing. Potential members of Parliament do not have to live in the constituency they wish to represent.

The night Margaret Roberts was adopted by Dartford she was driven to the train station afterward by a local party member named Denis Thatcher. Denis was ten years older than Margaret and a decorated war veteran. He had been briefly married during the war, but amicably divorced right afterward. For Denis Thatcher, this first meeting with Margaret Roberts was love at first sight. Margaret had other things on her mind, but she and Denis got on well. They shared the same political convictions, and Denis was quite knowledgeable about chemistry, since he ran his family's large paint and chemicals business. Margaret and Denis continued to see each other.

In order to be closer to her Dartford constituency, Margaret changed jobs. She found a position testing food products for the J. Lyons Company in London and moved to Dartford. The next months were filled with activity as Margaret settled into a new job and spent every free moment canvassing her district. Somehow Denis managed to keep on being a part of Margaret's life, partly by accompanying her to political meetings and other engagements. Denis Thatcher was a persistent man.

As expected, Margaret lost the by-election to the longtime Labour incumbent, but she had cut his majority considerably and was therefore considered a success. She lost again in the 1951 general election by an even narrower margin, although her party won. But her loss in 1951 was balanced by some happy things that were going on in her private life.

Denis Thatcher had been competing for Margaret's attention with a doctor who also could see her only if he tagged along on her canvassing or speaking engagements. It was probably harder for the doctor to keep up with her hectic schedule than it was for Denis Thatcher, the private businessman. In any case, Margaret and Denis announced their engagement in October 1951 and were married on December 13 that year.

By marrying Denis, Margaret Roberts took another giant step away from her roots in Grantham. Oxford had given her a first step up the social ladder. Marriage to Denis moved her firmly into the upper middle class. Denis came from a well-to-do family. He had gone to the most prestigious schools and was at home in all social circles. He shared her interests but had no political ambitions of his

The year was 1951 and Great Britain was still recovering from World War II. Margaret Roberts, then twenty-six years old, campaigned for the right to represent Dartford in Parliament. She lost in the election.

own. Instead, he was delighted to support and further hers. Now there were no financial obstacles to Margaret's dreams. Studying law, running for office—everything would be immeasurably easier.

Alfred Roberts, with his strict religious beliefs, could not have been totally happy about his daughter's marriage to a divorced man. But by now Margaret was independent enough to disregard parental disapproval, just as she had defied her father's teetotaling teachings when she gave sherry parties at Oxford. The wedding was held at Wesley's Chapel in London, a Methodist church. Many Conservative notables from the Dartford area attended, and the reception was held at the home of the Kent County Council president. It was the middle of winter, with postwar fuel shortages still in effect, and Margaret sensibly wore a long-sleeved, sapphire blue velvet dress, which had been copied from a painting by portrait painter Sir Joshua Reynolds.

After a short honeymoon to the Madeira Islands and to Portugal and Paris, the newlyweds settled into Denis Thatcher's flat in the Chelsea section of London. For the 1950s, it was a very modern marriage. In those days most women gave up their jobs to devote themselves to home, social life, and motherhood. But Margaret was not about to give up her political ambitions. Denis, in turn, encouraged her to continue her law studies, which she had begun earlier on a part-time basis. His work required irregular hours and a great deal of traveling. The Thatchers arranged their married life around their busy schedules.

They wanted to have two children, preferably a boy and a girl. In her usual efficient way, Margaret complied with both requirements by giving birth to twins, Carol and Mark, in August 1953. Their birth came between her intermediate bar exams in May and her bar finals in December. Since the Thatchers could afford a nanny for the babies, motherhood did not slow Margaret's work toward her law degree. She passed her bar examinations in 1954.

Always sensible, Margaret Thatcher had originally chosen to specialize in patent law because that could tie in with her scientific training. Now that she was aiming more directly for a political career, she switched to tax law. She was interested in the financial side of politics and knew that knowledge of tax laws and government financial policies (fiscal policy) would be invaluable assets for an aspiring member of Parliament. She also felt that this field would ensure more regular working hours for a wife and mother. In

Margaret and Denis Thatcher on their wedding day, December 13, 1951.

fact, when she went to work for a firm of tax lawyers, she generally managed to get home in time for her children's baths and evening meal. At first, she had a hard time finding a place in a tax law firm. Tax law was still very much a man's profession in the 1950s, and law firms were reluctant to hire a married woman with children.

Carol and Mark Thatcher, twins of a busy mother.

The years between 1951 and 1959 were Margaret Thatcher's only years of moderately normal domestic life. The Thatchers moved several times, giving Margaret a chance to indulge in one of her hobbies—decorating homes. But while she tried to spend as much time with her children as possible, Carol and Mark had to learn about shared family life elsewhere. They were able to do this at the farm of their mother's sister, Muriel Cullen, where they often spent vacation time.

Meanwhile, Margaret continued her quest for a constituency that would adopt her as a candidate. Over the years she had many disappointments as she went on interviews without being chosen. Here, too, the fact that she was the mother of young children counted against her. Conservatives in those days firmly believed that a mother's place was in the home. But it was not in Margaret's nature to quit, and Denis encouraged her to continue the fight. Finally, in 1957, she was adopted by Finchley, a suburban community just northwest of London. The incumbent had announced his intention to retire, and when his seat was vacated, Margaret was free to accept. Finchley had always been a much safer Conservative seat than some of the others she had sought.

The Margaret Thatcher who campaigned in 1959 was a very different person from the inexperienced young Margaret Roberts who had canvassed Dartford in 1950. At thirty-four, though still young, she was a skilled, seasoned campaigner. As a housewife, mother, lawyer, and tax expert, she could address many different people's concerns. She looked better, too. In 1950 she was a rather dowdy young woman who was apt to wear too many ruffles and feathered hats. Now she was always well dressed in tailored business suits and matching accessories. Over the years, Denis Thatcher had taught his wife many things she had not learned in Grantham. Dressing suitably for various occasions may have been among them. Margaret was now firmly poised for success. She had the ability to absorb what she needed quickly and efficiently and make it her own.

In the by-election of October 1959, Margaret Thatcher won Finchley for the Conservative party by a margin of 16,260 votes. She joined 608 male and 17 other female MPs in the House of Commons.

CHAPTER

4

MEMBER OF PARLIAMENT

When Margaret Thatcher was nine, she indignantly insisted that luck had played no part when she won a prize at a poetry reading. Indeed, a mixture of stubborn consistency, brilliant maneuvering, and plain hard work have gotten her to the top. But a streak of luck throughout her career has also boosted her progress from time to time.

One such lucky break came when the brand-new MP from Finchley had barely taken her seat on the back benches in the House of Commons. The green leather-back benches are used by MPs who do not hold specific positions in the government or in the Opposition party. Some MPs languish for years on the back benches without ever getting noticed. Most bills presented to Parliament are public bills introduced by the government in power. But each year twenty private members bills can be introduced by MPs at large. The right to introduce a private member bill is won in a sort of lottery. As a new MP, Margaret Thatcher drew a low and lucky number, 2.

Often, MPs use private member bills to advance a pet project. Rarely do these bills become law. But Margaret Thatcher was asked by the Conservative leader to propose a bill that was important to the party. The bill concerned the right of journalists to attend local council meetings so that the public at large could know what went on in those frequently closed meetings.

Because the bill was close to the heart of journalists, Margaret Thatcher's maiden speech in the Commons was covered thoroughly by the media. She did not disappoint her listeners. In a well-written, concise twenty-seven-minute speech during which she hardly ever referred to notes, Mrs. Thatcher presented a clear and compelling case. She was praised and congratulated even by members of the Opposition, and the bill, after some revision, eventually became law. The new member from Finchley had been noticed by the Conservative leadership, and Margaret Thatcher was on her way.

Soon she was given other responsibilities. Prime Minister Harold Macmillan appointed her parliamentary secretary to the Ministry of Pensions in 1961. Her duties involved dealing with thousands of complaints and inquiries by social security recipients and helping to resolve the problems. Many MPs might have considered this a somewhat tedious job, but Margaret Thatcher, with her tax law background, was well prepared for the intricate, detailed work. In any case, it was a feather in her cap to have been made a junior minister after only a little more than a year in Commons.

In 1959, the Conservative party had been in power for about eight years. In many respects England was still on the same course that Clement Attlee had set in 1945. The various social programs put in place by Labour governments continued to flourish and

THE BRITISH PARTY SYSTEM

Before 1830	Certain members of Parliament were known as Whigs, others as Tories, depending on their political leanings.
1830s	Tories became known as Conservatives.
1850s	Liberal party formed with Whig support.
1852–1924	Liberals and Conservatives alternately running the government.
1924	Labour party wins more votes than Liberal party and runs government for ten months.
1925–1929	Liberals versus Conservatives (Labour party exists as minority party).
1929–1935	Labour versus Conservatives.
1935–1945	Coalition governments.
1945–present	Labour versus Conservatives.
1981	Social Democratic party (SDP) formed.
1983	SDP and Liberals join to form Alliance party.

There are a number of other minority parties in Great Britain, including the Scottish National and the Northern Ireland parties, but they are represented in the House of Commons by just a few seats. They are seated with members of the official Opposition party.

expand. Successive Conservative governments had been content to leave most of the basic welfare state provisions in effect. These included government grants to families, students, pensioners, and the unemployed. Labour had nationalized many industries in England. As a result, government had taken over the ownership and sometimes the management of companies after paying full compensation to the previous owners. Public utilities and service industries such as gas, telecommunications, and air service were among

In 1961 Margaret Thatcher was appointed Parliamentary secretary to the Ministry of Pensions. She had been in the House of Commons little more than a year.

the first to be nationalized. The national health care system was comprehensive and growing. Conservatives and Labour leaders differed about the amount of spending by the government, about tax rates, and about price and wage controls. But their differences were a matter of degree. Even Conservative leaders who deplored the speed with which England was moving toward a form of economic socialism believed that the British public would not stand for any significant reductions in their government benefits.

It is important to understand the difference between capitalism and socialism to see why governments have such a difficult time steering their ship of state on a steady course. Pure socialism is basically a system in which government owns all the principal means of production, such as factories and sources of raw materials, and decides what to produce and how much. In return, government takes care of people's needs, such as housing, health care, and retirement benefits. The people do their part by working hard to the best of their ability while being paid a wage adequate to their needs. There is no reward for a worker's extra effort because pure socialism strives for total equality.

In the real world this form of idealistic, theoretical socialism has never been fully achieved. Some of the Scandinavian countries, Sweden in particular, have come fairly close to making socialism work in a political democracy. Other countries, including the United States, have adopted some aspects of the socialist ideal in their social welfare systems. Often, unfortunately, attempts at introducing socialism have degenerated into communism, which combines the economic principles of socialism with the harsh political dictatorships found in the Soviet Union and China. Or else it results in national bankruptcy when governments are unable to feed, house, or clothe their people. Examples of the failure of socialism can be found in some former colonial nations. Such failure is often the result of mismanagement by government officials. In other cases, greedy individuals misdirect production and distribution and line their own pockets instead of looking after the nation. The workers in such a system often see no future in being enterprising, industrious, or inventive since they cannot benefit from their efforts.

Pure capitalism does not provide all the answers, either. It is based on the idea of unrestricted free enterprise. Under a system of free enterprise, demand, supply, and the people's desire to increase their own well-being result in a naturally balanced flow of goods, services, jobs, and profits. In an economy based on pure capitalism, theoretically, the harder you work, the greater will be your rewards. Individual producers will manufacture only those goods for which there is adequate demand at the optimum price. If demand drops off, prices will fall and producers will immediately shift to a more profitable product. Workers will likewise move on to other industries where their labor is in demand at higher wages.

No country has ever achieved this ideal form of capitalism. It presupposes total knowledge about supplies, prices, job opportunities, and wages everywhere on the part of both employers and employees. It also presupposes total mobility. It is an impossible dream. Factory workers in steel plants or on automobile assembly lines cannot suddenly shift to high-tech jobs in computer or service industries. Workers whose families have lived for generations in one part of the country cannot be easily uprooted to find job opportunities elsewhere. At least not in the short run.

Most so-called capitalistic Western countries have a mix of socialism and capitalism. Government provides a safety net of programs to help those who can't help themselves. In some cases, government owns the public utilities or transportation systems. A private economy also exists in which individual employers and workers try to find their way to the best possible level of supply, demand, prices, and wages.

A larger amount of socialism in the mix ensures greater equality in income but tends to discourage individual enterprise and innovation. In a predominantly free-enterprise system, the nation benefits from the fruits of individual risk-taking and investment, but at the cost of wide differences in individual incomes and standards of living.

THE WELFARE STATE

During World War II, the British government was forced to impose many restrictions and controls. People became accustomed to government management of resources and accepted many rules and regulations. England's political parties worked together to win the war. After the war, Winston Churchill continued some of these controls, even though he was a Conservative. Churchill believed that the government should provide people with a safety net *and* a ladder to climb upward toward a better life by their own efforts. The Labour party, however, later introduced large-scale social programs that collectively became known as the welfare state.

By the early 1960s, some Conservative members of Parliament worried that the government, by adding ever more social programs, was drifting closer to socialism. Margaret Thatcher was a member of this group. She had strong convictions about self-reliance, enterprise, and the dignity of hard work. She felt that, while Churchill's safety net was in place, the ladder to a better life had been withdrawn. As higher and higher taxes and more and more regulations were being imposed on the people who were expected to produce new wealth, England was sliding away from the leadership position it had once held in the world of commerce and industry.

Even today Mrs. Thatcher carries a yellowing clipping in her purse with a quotation from a speech by Abraham Lincoln. It strongly reflects her own beliefs: "You cannot strengthen the weak by weakening the strong.... You cannot help the poor by destroying the rich.... You cannot help men permanently by doing for them what they could and should do for themselves." It was then and is now an idea that motivates her in government service.

Of course, in the early 1960s Mrs. Thatcher was in no position to influence government management decisions. The key word among British leaders in those days was "consensus"—agreement. People with different opinions tried to compromise to reach a mutually acceptable middle ground. Policies needed to be shaped in such a way that the Opposition could come to terms with whatever small changes were made. Labour politicians found themselves in a similar position when they ran the government. "Middle-of-the-road" was another favorite phrase to describe the same situation.

The problem for some Conservative politicians was that, as Labour shifted more and more to the Left, the middle-of-the-road MPs also shifted to the Left. And, as Mrs. Thatcher told an interviewer years later, "Standing in the middle of the road is very dangerous. You can get knocked down by traffic from both sides."

In the meantime, Margaret Thatcher concentrated on social security and pension problems. The sluggish civil service system was particularly exasperating for her. She complained that the entrenched bureaucrats cared more for rules, regulations, and precedent than for finding solutions to problems. The public suffered as a result of the system's inefficiency.

In 1963, Harold Macmillan resigned as prime minister and was succeeded by Edward Heath. But the Conservative party lost the general election in 1964. As members of the Opposition, Tory ministers could no longer influence government policy. But the members of the shadow cabinet could challenge Labour officials in Parliament and present their own point of view. Above all, shadow ministers have to keep up to date on all matters so that they can resume active service at a moment's notice if necessary.

Mrs. Thatcher was now reduced to handling pensions for the shadow cabinet. Nevertheless, her career advanced. In 1966 she was shifted from one shadow position to another. First she became shadow minister of housing and land. Then she assumed a junior position at the Treasury where, with her public finance background, she became a knowledgeable member of the shadow Treasury team. In fact, until well into the middle of the 1970s, Thatcher confided to friends that her highest career ambition was to become chancellor of the Exchequer.

Nevertheless, Heath moved her again. In 1967 she served as shadow minister of fuel and power, later shifting to the shadow ministry of transportation. In 1969, she became shadow minister of education. Margaret Thatcher did not mind the frequent moves. They provided her with invaluable experience in government.

The 1960s were good years for the Thatcher family. The twins had outgrown their nanny and been sent off to fashionable boarding schools—Mark to Harrow and Carol to Queenswood. To provide for their children's vacations, the Thatchers moved to a large country home with tennis courts and a swimming pool. In the winter there were family skiing trips to Switzerland. Denis Thatcher had sold the family business for a good price to the Burma Oil Company and had accepted a high-level executive job as well. So, while his wife was busy with her ministerial duties, Denis was happily traveling around the world on important business. It was a life-style that suited them both. It isn't so clear whether it also suited their children, who saw little of their busy parents.

For Margaret, a deep regret during those happy years was that her parents could not share in the joys of her success. Alfred Roberts died in 1970, shortly before his daughter became an active government minister. Her mother had died years earlier, in 1961.

CABINET MINISTER

The Conservatives were returned to power in 1970, giving Mrs. Thatcher her first taste of being a real cabinet minister. Government officials who make decisions affect the lives of real people. A move that seems wise and logical on paper will often be seen very differently by those who are affected. When Mrs. Thatcher took over as minister of education, many proposals that had been prepared by her Labour predecessor were already in the planning stage. One she enacted was to cut free milk for schoolchildren above the age of eight. A firestorm of protest descended on her. Parents were outraged that a woman minister would deprive their children of their customary free milk. Protesters chanted slogans: "Maggie, Maggie Thatcher, the Milk Snatcher!"

The criticism over the free milk cuts devastated Mrs. Thatcher. It was one of her lowest moments in government service. She was a strong advocate of school improvements. In fact, while she preached less government spending, under her leadership the education budget, for the very first time, was larger than the defense budget. Among her ideas was the extension of preschool education to three- and four-year-olds so that underprivileged children could compete "on a level playing field" with middle-class children.

Another controversial move concerned the conversion of grammar schools into comprehensive secondary schools that offered academic and general education under one roof. The previous Labour government had tried to speed up the consolidation of grammar schools into comprehensive schools. Mrs. Thatcher rescinded that order. She was and has remained a strong supporter of the elitist grammar schools that separate the gifted from their less able schoolmates. To her mind, lumping all children together in a comprehensive school meant lowering standards. Freedom of choice has also been one of her major beliefs. As a result of these views, Mrs. Thatcher gave school districts the freedom to retain grammar schools if they pleased.

The movement toward comprehensive schools has continued. Today most English children attend such schools. Mrs. Thatcher would like to slow down or even reverse that trend. She remembers the value of her own grammar school experience with nostalgia.

Margaret Thatcher's stand on the grammar school question and the free milk fiasco embittered many people against the new minister of education.

Although Mrs. Thatcher was now a full-fledged member of the Heath cabinet, she did not belong to his inner circle. Heath had taken her into his cabinet as the token woman, but he did not like her very much, nor did he trust women in high office. At the cabinet table he placed her in an unfavorable position where she could never catch his eye. And although she loyally supported his positions while she was in his cabinet, Ted Heath knew that Margaret Thatcher disagreed with many of them. Deteriorating economic conditions and union pressures had forced Heath to move closer to the consensus-style, middle-of-the-road politics Thatcher and others were beginning to worry about.

In 1970 Great Britain was in decline. The downward trend had started shortly after World War II with the dismantling of Britain's colonial empire. Even though the former colonies were still loosely tied to Great Britain in the British Commonwealth, these now independent nations no longer served to enrich Great Britain. Important markets for British goods were lost, as were cheap sources of raw materials. Instead, immigrants from former colonies moved to Britain seeking jobs and a better way of life. The influx of newcomers created conflicts regarding housing and employment.

There were many other problems. The countries of Continental Western Europe had rebuilt their war-torn industries with modern plants and equipment. England lagged far behind with outdated factories and unproductive methods. The work force graduating from English schools could not compete with their better-trained and more highly motivated Continental European counterparts. The traditional leisurely pace and work habits of English workers and managers kept England behind other industrialized nations. Militant trade unions also aggravated the situation.

Some critics blamed a welfare-state mentality for the lack of enterprise, innovation, and individual ambition. Some blamed excessive taxes and the nationalization of industries for the decline in private entrepreneurship. Starting a new business, risking one's savings, and working very hard just didn't seem worthwhile.

The biggest problem was the monstrous increase in public expenditures. The welfare-state benefits were costly and had to be paid for somehow. At first, the money came from the wealthy in ever rising tax rates, but gradually taxes also had to increase for the middle classes. In some ways, those government benefits were not as free as they had seemed at first. An ever-growing share of the population paid for these benefits with their taxes and had no say in how their money was to be spent.

There were many discussions about public finance during Thatcher's first years as a cabinet minister. Her advice was not often asked, but she had strong opinions. She believed that governments had to live within a budget just as families had to control their spending. Of course, there is a big difference between a family's budget and a government's. While a family can occasionally bridge a bad moment by getting credit in a store or borrowing from a bank, these loans are usually of brief duration and have to be repaid on time. Governments, on the other hand, have vast borrowing powers. Their loans can be turned over and over again when they come due. Governments also have a second but more dangerous tool to increase their supply of money: the power to print more money.

When a government prints too much money, the value of the money declines. When a government borrows too much money, it has to pay more and more money in interest to the lenders. When a government spends more money than it takes in through taxes, it is forced to borrow, and the result is what we call a deficit. Printing money and borrowing to pay for government expenditures serves to pump more money into people's hands. Raising taxes takes away spending money. Taxing, borrowing, and spending at the right moment and in the right proportions is a complicated juggling act. A country can either slide into a slump or overheat into inflation. The latter happens when too much money is chasing too few goods or services and prices are driven up.

Economics used to be a branch of philosophy. Economists gravely discussed various theories and made predictions about their effects. Some people today consider economics a science. The problem is that the economists' laboratory is the country at large. Politicians are the lab assistants. If an experiment goes wrong in a real laboratory, the damage is limited. But in the laboratory of a nation's economy, a faulty theory will immediately affect millions of people. Wages and prices may shoot up, factories may be forced to close, and people may be out of work.

Supply and demand graphs tell manufacturers that they can sell only so many widgets at any given price and that they must stop production when demand no longer exists. But what can you do when the product in oversupply happens to be people trained for an outdated industry? You can't eliminate all those unemployable people.

No wonder politicians hate to make decisions involving major changes in taxes, government spending, and interest rates. The results are usually unpredictable and most likely very unpopular. It requires a strong and confident leader to switch course and to make decisions that may be harsh and unpopular in the short run.

Edward Heath was not a strong leader. He had championed ideas that would curb union power and reduce government spending, but he pulled back when the Opposition went on the attack. Heath made a U-turn, as Margaret Thatcher charged at a later time. Many members of his cabinet became increasingly uncomfortable when he gave in to Labour pressures about continued price and wage controls. In spite of his conciliatory attempts to get along with the unions, England was plagued by labor troubles.

In 1974 Heath called for early elections with the slogan, "Who runs the country—the government or the unions?" The Conservatives lost marginally, and Heath tried to remain in power by attempting to engineer a coalition with the Liberals. He did not succeed. Harold Wilson, the Labour leader, was asked by the queen to form a new government, even though Labour did not command a majority in Parliament. Trying to improve that condition, Wilson called for new elections in October 1974, and Labour won a narrow victory.

The defeat of Edward Heath set in motion a series of events that eventually would propel one of the more obscure members of his cabinet to become his most unlikely rival and successor. The ascent of Margaret Hilda Thatcher to the pinnacle of the Conservative party in the space of one short year is a tale of misjudgments, miscalculations, intrigue, and perhaps the misperception that a woman couldn't possibly be a serious contender.

5

TWO GIANT STEPS FOR MARGARET THATCHER

After the Conservative defeat, in the forced February election and again in the general election in October 1974, it took five years and two major steps to propel Mrs. Thatcher from the shadow ministry of education through the black-lacquered door of Number 10 Downing Street. The Conservatives certainly hoped to regain control of the government. Many believed they should be led by someone other than twice-defeated Edward Heath. But if anyone had bet on the names of possible new leaders, Mrs. Thatcher's name certainly would not have been on the list.

Some members of Parliament, including several members of the Heath cabinet, felt that the gentlemanly thing for Edward Heath to do would be to resign his leadership position. He had been challenged twice in one year by Labour and had lost both times. Heath had become something of an embarrassment to the Conservative party. In less democratic times he might have been removed through behind-the-scenes maneuvering. But the Conservative party had adopted new and somewhat more open rules. Leaders had to be reelected yearly by their own MPs. If Heath could not be persuaded to resign, his leadership would have to be challenged.

And that was the rub. English politicians educated in the best-known public schools and imbued with the gentlemanly rules of cricket and rugby, with the concepts of fair play and loyalty, found it very difficult to challenge a leader who did not want to quit. One after another the cabinet members with the most experience and the greatest sympathies for what Heath had tried to achieve pledged that they would not oppose him on the first leadership ballot. Most of these loyalists believed that Heath would win anyway. If not, they expected scattered results that would require a second ballot. Time enough, then, for one of these leading candidates to step forward and claim the prize.

Among those in the right wing of the Conservative party who definitely wanted a change of leadership were several very able potential leaders. Mrs. Thatcher who, by the early 1970s, definitely counted herself among the right-wingers, supported Sir Keith Joseph, from whom she had learned much about economic policy. But Sir Keith took himself effectively out of the running when he gave an ill-advised and clumsily worded speech in which he inadvertently came across as both a sexist and a racist. Other right-wing challengers also gradually dropped out of the fight. It was at this point that an old friend of Mrs. Thatcher's encouraged her to enter the ring. Airey Neave had known Thatcher when they both worked in the same law firm, and they had been back-bench colleagues in the Commons. Neave had no leadership ambitions of his own, but he hoped to influence events by being someone else's campaign manager. Thatcher was not Airey's first choice as leader. He originally hoped to manage the leadership contest for not one but two other potential candidates. But when those choices could not be sustained, he turned to Mrs. Thatcher as a kindred soul.

It was a daring gamble. Mrs. Thatcher was still basically an outsider even though she had been entrusted with many different shadow cabinet positions. Even after losing in February, Edward Heath continued to move her around his shadow cabinet. He installed her as environment minister and asked her to design a new housing policy. He also increased her visibility by making her his spokesperson for Treasury affairs. Although Heath didn't like Mrs. Thatcher, he appreciated her abilities. Loyal to him until now, Mrs. Thatcher had nevertheless taken definite steps in more recent years to distance herself from some of his policies. She had joined Keith Joseph and others in a newly formed study group called the Center for Political Studies. She eventually became the president of this group, although Sir Keith remained the guiding light. The study group competed in many ways with the party research organization, which served to guide the policies set by Heath. Mrs. Thatcher had never hidden her disenchantment with consensus politics and with the current state of economic management. And in spite of her longtime role as a loyal team player, she didn't suffer from the "gentlemanly" handicaps of the public schools and playing fields of England. Once some of the people she admired had stepped aside, Mrs. Thatcher had no qualms about standing up against the man who had treated her rather badly for many years.

Someone had to oppose Edward Heath on the first ballot, and many of those who now rallied around Mrs. Thatcher secretly felt that she was a safe choice. No one believed that she could win on the first ballot, and no one believed that Heath would win a clear majority either. So the stage was set for one of the "real" future leaders to enter the fight in the second round.

The people who created this situation—and they did not include Airey Neave—certainly didn't understand Margaret Thatcher. They didn't understand that, when she fought a battle, she fought to win. They certainly underestimated the power of her beliefs and her ability to get her ideas across in clear, simple language and impassioned appeals. Her audience, in this case, was made up of the backbenchers who had been ignored and pushed aside by Edward Heath and his favored insiders. But the backbenchers had a vote in the leadership election. To the astonishment of everyone, except perhaps Margaret and Denis Thatcher, Mrs. Thatcher won 130 votes against 119 for Heath on the first ballot, with 16 additional votes for a token outsider. For the second ballot, a number of the original favorites entered the contest. But too many came in, and they entered too late. Margaret Thatcher won a clear victory with 146 votes while only 79 votes were cast for her nearest competitor. The long-ignored backbenchers had registered their disenchantment with the inside leadership quite clearly at the ballot box. One of Margaret Thatcher's biographers, Hugo Young, called this "the revolt of the peasants." In Margaret Thatcher, the "peasants" had found a spokesperson and a champion.

CONSERVATIVE LEADER

Thatcher's elevation to the Conservative leadership was not easy on her husband and children. Her work schedule soared. Her hours were erratic. They, along with her, were transfixed in a glare of publicity. Denis Thatcher continued to support his wife, but it couldn't have been an easy role to play for an active and successful business executive used to making his own decisions and scheduling his own life. Now he often had to plan his schedule around his wife's. The Thatchers had sold their country home in 1970 and moved back to London to a small red-brick house in Chelsea. It had been another chance for Margaret to indulge in her passion for interior decorating. Painting, wallpapering, and choosing new color schemes and furnishings helped her relax and gave her an outlet for her creative energies. But now, as the leader of the Conservative party, she had more serious things on her mind.

The leadership election in February 1975 marked Mrs. Thatcher's first giant step in the direction of Downing Street. But

Mrs. Thatcher relaxes by decorating, painting, and cooking. Here, she and daughter Carol wallpaper.

the road ahead was long and hazardous. The Labour party was firmly in control, although their last victory had been very narrow. And among Margaret's Conservative colleagues, few believed she could last long as party leader. Her election had been a fluke, they felt, and the next leadership contest would set matters right and put one of the insiders in control of the party again.

Mrs. Thatcher, however, had matters firmly in hand. She had no illusions about the obstacles in her path. She knew she had to hold on to her leadership position within her own party and persuade her peers that the old policy of consensus and compromise needed to be replaced. She also had to persuade the country that her policies and ideas were better than those of the Labour party and that England needed to return to Tory rule. It was an enormous challenge, but Margaret Thatcher was ready for the fight.

Her approach was two-pronged. Within her party, she proceeded with caution and conciliation. She kept a majority of Heath loyalists in her shadow cabinet and held out the olive branch of peace to Heath himself by offering him the post of ambassador to the United States or a place in her shadow cabinet. Heath brusquely refused her offers. He took her challenge to his leadership as a personal betrayal, and he never forgave her. He remained in Parliament as a sullen backbencher. The other Conservative MPs, however, agreed to work with Margaret Thatcher. Since she didn't make any radical changes but sought their cooperation and advice, many of them gradually became her allies. To work with a cabinet in which she and her political mentors were, in fact, in the minority required wisdom, patience, and a long-range view of how her own philosophy could be applied. She knew what she wanted, but she also knew that time was on her side. With persistence and endurance, she and her policies could win. Sadly, one of her staunchest supporters, Airey Neave, was assassinated by the Irish Republican Army (IRA) shortly after the leadership election. The death of Neave was a blow to Margaret Thatcher. It also served to personalize her already strong feelings about the terrorist activities of some Irish nationalists. Mrs. Thatcher was strongly criticized for her harsh stand when a number of IRA members died during a hunger strike in prison. But she has felt strongly that political aims do not justify the taking of innocent lives.

Her stance toward the Opposition was very different. Thatcher, the outsider and token cabinet minister, suddenly became very visible across the country as Conservative party leader. Day after day she stridently challenged Labour in speeches within the halls of Parliament and in interviews with the media.

HER MESSAGE

Mrs. Thatcher's message was loud and clear. England was in decline, she said, not only economically but also socially and morally. To put the "Great" back into Great Britain, the country needed to go back to the Victorian values of thrift, order, duty, efficiency, and individual responsibility. She blasted socialism for depriving individuals of their rights to make choices, to accept responsibility for themselves. "Individually, man is creative;" she said, "collectively, he tends to be a spendthrift." She felt that the failing of socialism was the belief that government can take charge of what should be an individual's own sense of responsibility. Instead, this assumption has led to individual irresponsibility and selfishness.

"Moral responsibility will not keep going if the government steps in and makes all the decisions for you, decisions you ought to make for yourself," she said.

"People have forgotten about the personal society," she told an interviewer. She felt strongly that people were important, that they needed a sense of self-worth. It was her aim to leave more tax money in people's hands so that they could make more decisions for themselves. "Presenting people with opportunities is what politics is all about," she said.

She argued that while socialism and communism give privileges to a few people at the top and none to the many, capitalism really works only "by spreading ever more widely to more and more of the population what used to be the privileges of the few."

Some people accused Mrs. Thatcher of spreading her message

with almost evangelical zeal in those years. Of course, the message was the one she had learned at her father's knee during her Grantham childhood. Victorian virtues and individual responsibilities were the teachings of the Methodist lay preacher who had shaped her thinking and her sense of mission.

She convinced many people. The back-bench rank-and-filers supported her each year at the leadership elections. Many ordinary people came to regard her as their champion, fighting for the individual, trying to curb the power of union bosses in relation to their powerless members, and attempting to reduce the power of government in its role as landlord, tax collector, and general oppressor.

Mrs. Thatcher energetically joined battle with the union bosses. Already in 1974 the Tories had campaigned under the slogan "Who runs the government?" because of the ever-growing influence of trade unions over the Labour party. Officers of the TUC (Trade Union Council) were constant visitors to Number 10 Downing Street. Over the years the unions in England had gained a stranglehold on manufacturing, on price- and wage-setting policies, and on where and when people could work. In 1974, voters had returned the country to Labour control partly out of a conviction that the Labour party had more influence over the union bosses. It didn't turn out that way. As the oil shortages of the late 1970s drove up prices, unions became ever more strident in their demands for higher wages.

Margaret Thatcher argued for free collective bargaining—that is, plant managers and union representatives freely settling their differences without government control and interference. Edward Heath had believed that free bargaining would put even more pressure on inflation by driving up wages in an uncontrolled way. He had sided with the Labour party in support of price and wage controls. In 1979, James Callaghan, the Labour prime minister, tried desperately to limit wage increases in the face of growing labor unrest, but his union friends let him down. Strikes broke out

In the election of 1979, Margaret Thatcher was able to convince ordinary people that she was their champion. She succeeded.

all over. People were sick and tired of the inconveniences caused by frequent wildcat strikes in coal mining and transportation. Even health care facilities were victims of strikes. In a self-protective move, doctors had begun to unionize. Parents found their children locked out of school when teachers went on strike. There were shortages of fuel, power outages, and other hardships as many companies were forced to cut back to a three-day week.

James Callaghan had survived one no-confidence challenge thrown at him in Parliament by Mrs. Thatcher, with help from the Liberal party. At one time the Liberal party had been Great Britain's major Opposition party, but it had lost many members to the Tories and to Labour. In 1979, Mrs. Thatcher challenged Callaghan again, and for the first time in over fifty years, a government was defeated in a vote of no confidence, triggering new elections in May.

Still, few people believed that Mrs. Thatcher would prevail over the Labour party, even though that party was now in disarray. As election results were being tallied late into the night on May 3,

1979, and into the early morning hours of May 4, Mrs. Thatcher nervously cleaned and straightened drawers in her Chelsea house. A small crisis developed when one of the ballot boxes from her own Finchley district could not be found for a while. It would have been absurd for her to lose her own safe district due to such a silly mishap. By 3:00 A.M. on May 4, it was clear that a Conservative triumph had been assured. The Thatchers made a quick visit to Conservative headquarters to receive cheers and congratulations. The miracle had happened. Margaret Thatcher had led her party to victory!

The Thatchers went back to headquarters again at noon the next day to enjoy champagne toasts and a huge chocolate cake decorated to look like the black door to Number 10 Downing Street. Then came the tense wait for the call from Buckingham Palace, which could come only after James Callaghan had visited the queen to hand in his resignation.

For Margaret Thatcher, her forty-five minute audience with the queen must have seemed like the pinnacle on her long upward climb from Grantham. For Denis, it meant a long wait in the company of Prince Philip, the queen's husband.

And then it was done. Before entering Number 10 Downing Street, Mrs. Thatcher paused to offer a prepared quotation attributed by some to Saint Francis of Assisi. " 'Where there is discord, may we bring harmony,' " she said. " 'Where there is error, may we bring truth. Where there is doubt, may we bring faith. Where there is despair, may we bring hope.' " The words were probably addressed as much to herself as to her audience of reporters, television camera crews, and onlookers. In her own mind she was a woman with a mission. That mission was to halt England's slide into socialism and to reverse its path. She had no illusions about how difficult a task she had set for herself.

6

THE HONORABLE LADY

A woman prime minister of Great Britain! The news caused a sensation around the world. Even though people had plenty of warning that it could happen, the public simply hadn't seriously considered that it would. Yet for four years Margaret Thatcher had prepared for the job. She led the Conservative party, made speeches, attacked the Labour party, and traveled around the globe to meet foreign leaders.

All new prime ministers face the difficult task of forming a new cabinet, asserting authority, formulating new policies, and persuading the government to follow their lead. For the first female prime minister in British history, this task became immeasurably more difficult. The doubts and obstacles Mrs. Thatcher faced are those encountered by most women in leadership positions. Many questions were asked. Could a woman represent British interests forcefully at international meetings? Could she control a cabinet made up of strong and experienced political leaders, many of whom had their own agendas and ideas? Did an attractive and feminine woman really have what it took to manage the affairs of a major nation?

Mrs. Thatcher was not the first woman to hold such an important position. Golda Meir of Israel and Indira Gandhi of India were able and forceful heads of state. But Israel and India are not major world powers. And Great Britain stood at a turning point in 1979. The following years would be decisive in determining whether it could regain its stature as a leader among nations. Was Mrs. Thatcher capable of turning Great Britain's fate around?

She had, in fact, answered many of these questions during her years as Conservative party leader. She had clearly stated her aims, her approach, and her programs. She had proved her toughness abroad with a strongly anti-communist speech delivered on a visit to the Soviet Union. Some of her Conservative colleagues thought the speech was undiplomatic, rash, and ill-considered. The Soviet news agency Tass labeled her "the Iron Lady." The nickname stuck and Mrs. Thatcher rather liked it. "Britain needs an Iron Lady," she said. Since then, the woman who was thought to lack foreign-policy experience when she first entered Downing Street has put Britain back on the map in international councils. She is now considered a major world leader. She is certainly the most experienced among the current Western leaders.

Mrs. Thatcher stood up to the members of her cabinet as well. In some ways she had them at a disadvantage. Brought up to be polite and chivalrous to ladies, the cabinet members found it difficult to spar with the woman who now sat at the head of the table. In addition, Mrs. Thatcher's love for debating, nurtured since her grammar school days and honed to perfection at Oxford, tended to turn ordinary discussions into encounters between adversaries. The men who were supposed to be her advisers rather than her opponents often found her approach exhausting. Her style of running cabinet meetings was different, too. She was impatient with long-winded discussions that did not lead to quick solutions. She came to the meetings with her own agenda and expected her cabinet to help her implement her programs. "Tell me *how*," she told them, "I know *what*." Predictably, they didn't like the approach, and with reason. Mrs. Thatcher did not adopt the expected cabinet conventions. She was apt to cut off debates in the middle or to rebuff cabinet ministers by making informal deals behind their backs. She acted, some complained, like a forceful managing director of a company rather than like a kindly chairperson of the board who oversees, moderates, and listens, but doesn't bother with details.

Mrs. Thatcher thrives on details. In her first term as prime minister, she visited every government department, shaking up the civil service managers who had never been so closely overseen. Her Downing Street staff was amazed to find that the prime minister always did her homework. She worked through every paper in the leather dispatch boxes in which reports, documents, and proposals were delivered to her daily, annotating them with comments and queries blue-penciled in the margins. Her staff was also unused to such close supervision.

To everyone's surprise, and in spite of dire predictions, Mrs. Thatcher's programs, plans, and way of doing things generally prevailed. The Iron Lady couldn't be stopped, not by unhappy cabinet officers, not by public opinion, an entrenched bureaucracy, or civil service opposition.

People are still surprised by Mrs. Thatcher. Somehow, in spite of her three election victories and the fact that she has been able to implement most of her program, Mrs. Thatcher's skill as a politician is still underestimated.

POWERS OF THE PRIME MINISTER

Mrs. Thatcher was able to do so much because a British prime minister, in many ways, has greater powers than an American president. Almost all legislation enacted in Parliament is introduced by the government in power. This means that bills are sponsored, or at least approved, by the prime minister. And the prime minister expects support as a matter of party discipline. American presidents, on the other hand, must compete with both houses of Congress for the introduction of bills before the legislature. If the president's party does not control Congress, he or she may not prevail.

There are other important differences. British prime ministers must present themselves twice a week to Parliament for a traditional question period. During this meeting the Opposition, and sometimes members of the ruling party, are free to challenge the prime minister on any subject at all. Twice a week Margaret Thatcher spends long hours preparing for that onslaught. The question period is a free-for-all when tempers flare and voices rise. Mrs. Thatcher had to learn to outshout her opponents without letting her voice become shrill.

The questioning sessions are open to the press. American presidents grant press conferences only as frequently, or as infrequently, as they desire. The American press's freedom to question presidents is much more limited, and the reporters' manner is more restrained.

A prime minister is rarely defeated on major bills. A defeat would mean that many members of his or her own party did not support the measure. A defeat could even lead to a vote of no confidence and possibly new elections. American presidents have greater job security. They can count on staying in office for at least four years!

The British cabinet differs from the American cabinet, too. American presidents choose the members of their cabinets from among able people in the country at large. Often American cabinet members are longtime friends and advisers of the president. They might be men and women who have distinguished themselves in industry, education, financial institutions, or government. But

November 1981. Mrs. Thatcher leads her cabinet from the House of Commons into the House of Lords for the opening of Parliament. The benches used by MPs are shown to the left and to the right.

while these cabinet members, who must be approved by Congress, advise the president and run the various governmental departments they head, they are strictly members of the executive branch. They have no political power of their own and no voice in Congress.

The British prime minister's cabinet has to be chosen from among members of Parliament. These are people trusted by the prime minister. Presumably, they share the prime minister's views of how the country should be governed. They advise the PM and actively help formulate policy. In addition, cabinet ministers can forcefully promote their policies on the floor of Parliament and cast their own votes in favor of the bill.

Margaret Thatcher did not always have this kind of support during her first term in office. After all, she had cautiously retained many of the ministers who served Edward Heath. They frequently accused Thatcher of high-handedness. "Presidential" and "imperial" were words some cabinet ministers used to describe Mrs. Thatcher's treatment of her cabinet. In turn, she labeled those cabinet members who seemed too cautious, too middle-of-the-road, and too consensus-minded as "wet," probably meaning "wrong." The label stuck and certain factions in her government are still known as the "Wets" today. Naturally, the people who favored Mrs. Thatcher's policies, people she considered innovative and fearless, became known as the "Drys." She herself refers to any person who shares her views as "one of us."

People who know her well report that the "real" Mrs. Thatcher is neither as tough nor as self-assured as she seems. In her early days as prime minister, she often suffered from great self-doubt, but she needed to appear strong and certain if she wanted to assert her authority. Now well into her third term in office, she has assembled a group of cabinet ministers who share her views and convictions. She no longer needs to dominate or to assert herself so forcefully. Success has its rewards.

Nevertheless, the image of the Iron Lady remains. Perhaps Mrs. Thatcher herself admires the qualities of leadership and dominance often labeled "male" and has felt compelled to adopt such traits in her role as a political leader. She often sounds harsh and severe, and from the beginning political leaders and the public have often regarded her as an "honorary man," as if her leadership qualities could only be explained by saying that she isn't really like a woman! To the dismay of feminists, Mrs. Thatcher hasn't strongly rejected that point of view. For example, she accepted honorary membership in the all-male Carlton Club to which every previous prime minister had been elected.

WOMAN AND LEADER

However much she proved her toughness and capability, Mrs. Thatcher's critics wouldn't forget that she was a woman. It is interesting that, in a country that has adored its current queen for almost four decades and has dealt with strong queens in the past, the existence of a female political leader should stir up so much anxiety and interest. Some of the criticism of Mrs. Thatcher was indirect. When she raised her voice in Parliament—a place famous for shouted exchanges—she was accused of sounding like a "fishwife." When she got the better of an opponent, she was reported to have "handbagged" the unfortunate foe. Comments were made about her clothes, her hair, her voice. Some of them were quite vicious.

"A working-class Tory with beehive hairdo, and with the kind of suppressed vowel problems that would require the services of Eliza Doolittle's Professor Higgins," one of her detractors wrote in *Harper's Magazine* in 1985. This was published after Mrs. Thatcher was denied an honorary degree by Oxford University, an honor almost automatically bestowed on any prime minister with an Oxford degree. Thatcher was, in fact, only the third person to be denied the degree after such an honor had been proposed. (The others were President Harry Truman of the United States and Prime Minister Zulfikar Ali Bhutto of Pakistan.) Mrs. Thatcher was cold-shouldered by Oxford partly because her government cut university funds and many students lost their grants. Although students do not have a vote in the granting of honorary doctorates, half of the Oxford student body signed a petition asking that the honor be denied.

Mrs. Thatcher herself has contributed to the public's preoccupation with her feminine qualities. Perhaps in self-defense, she has made many quips about the superiority of women as leaders and managers. She has quoted the Greek philosopher Sophocles: "Once a woman is made equal to a man, she becomes his superior." "Women tend to be very much more practical, less theoretical," she told an interviewer. "They look much more to the long term because they are concerned about the world into which their children will grow . . . they are managers in their homes. They have the experience of making decisions and not passing the buck." And in a different context she has said, "If you want something said, ask a man. If you want something done, ask a woman." This kind of statement might have led people to believe that Mrs. Thatcher would encourage other women to enter the male-dominated field of politics. Members of the women's movement in England have been disappointed that she hasn't done so. In her more than ten years as prime minister, Mrs. Thatcher has taken only one other woman into her cabinet, Baroness Janet Young, who was the leader of the House of Lords from 1981 to 1983. Some critics have maliciously suggested that there are no other woman in her cabinet because Mrs. Thatcher likes being the only woman surrounded by men in all those cabinet group photos. Leaders of militant women's groups have criticized her for stressing her "masculine" leadership qualities on one hand and extolling feminine virtues on the other. They have also deplored the fact that her budget cuts and her emphasis on individual initiative have deprived poor working mothers of government support they need in their struggle to raise their children and keep their jobs. How much can overburdened women realistically do for themselves? the women ask.

Margaret Thatcher herself has dismissed the women's movement. "What have they ever done for me?" she asked during a press conference in 1975. In fact, Mrs. Thatcher has done much for women. She has proved that a woman can meet men on equal terms and that she can do so while remaining feminine.

Mrs. Thatcher clearly enjoys dressing well, and it is hard to understand why she is criticized for trying to look better. She feels it is important for a woman politician to look her best, and she has worked on her appearance, changing her hairstyle, choosing the best colors for her clothes, and learning to lower her voice. If, in her private moments, she enjoys cooking meals for her husband or redecorating the state apartments in Downing Street, this doesn't diminish her accomplishments as a prime minister. Nobody ever criticized a male prime minister for enjoying a game of golf or tennis or being interested in rugby or horse racing. Decorating is still one of Mrs. Thatcher's favorite hobbies. A wonderful picture appears in a magazine article written by Carol Thatcher about her mother. In the photograph, the prime minister is standing on a ladder, helping to wallpaper her daughter's new apartment. She is wearing a dress, stockings, high heels and, as the only concession to what she is doing, a scarf over her hair.

Early in her career, Mrs. Thatcher was dismayed by the "Milk Snatcher" nickname. There have been many other nicknames since then. Critics have called her "Attila the Hen," rather admiring her toughness. A more endearing name is "Nanny Thatcher."

In some ways that's how the British public sees her—a strict but loving disciplinarian—part mother, part headmistress, part nurse. Mary Poppins, the fictional nanny, gave her charges a spoonful of sugar to make the medicine go down. There was very little sugar at first to go with the medicine that Nanny Thatcher prescribed for the British public. There was, in fact, a lot of bitter medicine in the programs she proposed during her first term in office. Mrs. Thatcher's strong measures led inevitably to higher unemployment, lower wages, and a great deal of dislocation as parts of the welfare state were dismantled. But there were rewards as well. The Thatcher government saw to it that millions of public "council" houses were sold to their tenants at affordable prices. Many government-owned industries were privatized, giving the public the opportunity to buy stock. Millions of working people suddenly owned their homes and shares of stock for the first time in their lives. These new homeowners and recently made capitalists became supporters of Mrs. Thatcher. They now share her dream of a Britain in which everyone will have a financial stake in the nation's success.

Margaret Thatcher believes in strong medicine. "After almost any operation," she told an interviewer, "you feel worse before you convalesce [recover]. But you do not refuse the operation." Many people in Britain seem to agree.

She went a long way with her "conviction" program (as opposed to the "consensus" system embraced by her predecessors) during her first term. She did so in spite of her narrow victory and the fact that she had won a smaller share of the popular vote than any previous prime minister with a comparable parliamentary majority in recent times. In British elections it is the number of parliamentary seats won by the party that counts. In a somewhat similar way, U.S. presidents could theoretically win enough electoral votes state by state even if they lose in the popular vote. Of course, in British elections the name of the future prime minister isn't actually on any ballot. People vote for a party, understanding very well, however, who will be leading that party and what the leader stands for.

Mrs. Thatcher prevailed because she understood how to present her case to the rank-and-file MPs and to certain sections of the general public. She wasn't exactly popular—some say she has been the most unpopular prime minister in recent times—but people understood what she was trying to do and gave her a chance to try a new approach.

At election time her admirers shouted, "Maggie Thatcher is the best man we have," and women raised placards reading "Maggie Is Our Man." Foreign leaders have been quick to recognize her strong will. She stood up for Great Britain at European Community (EC) meetings, complaining that England was being shortchanged by the other European nations. "I want my money," she told the assembled leaders. She won her point. And she found a flexible approach to the tricky situation facing Great Britain in strife-torn Rhodesia (present-day Zimbabwe) by standing up to the British settlers in that African nation and thus making a compromise solution possible.

There is another side to the tough, aggressive prime minister. People who actually meet Mrs. Thatcher often comment on her charm, graciousness, and lack of pretension. In her gold and white Downing Street office, she offers tea to her guests, plumps up their pillows, and makes sure they are comfortable. The office once had hideous green flocked wallpaper and heavy furniture, which Mrs. Thatcher replaced at her own expense at the start of her second term. She has enhanced other state rooms as well by borrowing from various London museums. Even the silverware used for state dinners is on loan.

Paying for the refurbishing of her office was a generous gesture, particularly since Mrs. Thatcher has refused to accept the full prime minister's salary of about $100,000. Instead, she takes only the $80,000 a year paid to other cabinet ministers. It is her personal way to underscore the need for less government spending.

Mrs. Thatcher is gracious to interviewers and guests and also takes a caring, concerned attitude toward her staff. She remembers names of wives, husbands, and children and offers taxi rides home to women staff members who have to work late at night. Mrs. Thatcher refuses to employ sleep-in domestic staff for her private quarters because, with her irregular hours, it would mean keeping servants up late. Instead, she often cooks quick meals for herself and Denis as late as eleven or twelve.

She works late into the night but then is up at six, fixing eggs and bacon for Denis and black coffee and grapefruit for herself. She listens to the news on the radio and skims the morning papers

As prime minister, Mrs. Thatcher must read numerous reports, analyze them, and form responses. Margaret Thatcher often works late into the night on her dispatch boxes, actually suitcases, which contain important papers.

while having breakfast. There isn't a wasted moment in her day. The Grantham girl who could compress four years of Latin into one still has the ability to absorb huge amounts of complex information in an amazingly brief time. When evening meetings with cabinet members drag on far into the night, Mrs. Thatcher sometimes whips up a quick meal for her colleagues so that not a moment is lost.

The pace is sometimes too hectic for Denis Thatcher. At social gatherings, he occasionally rescues overwhelmed guests by signaling Margaret to slow down. Sometimes when the political discussion overwhelms him, he withdraws and lets the politicians carry on. For relaxation, the Thatchers spend time at Chequers, a government-owned country estate reserved for the use of prime ministers. Here, the Thatchers frequently entertain important foreign guests, cabinet members, and members of the staff. For Mrs. Thatcher, a moment of relaxation means reading a spy novel, or watching tapes of her favorite television show, "Yes, Minister." She enjoys music, particularly opera, and is an avid collector of Crown Derby china.

Reporting to the monarch is one of the responsibilities of the prime minister. Mrs. Thatcher and Queen Elizabeth II attend a party for the leaders of the Commonwealth nations.

One of her most important tasks is her weekly private audience with the queen. It must be an interesting encounter. Mrs. Thatcher is the eighth prime minister to report to Queen Elizabeth II in the almost forty years of the monarch's reign. Previous prime ministers were often elderly gentlemen who brought a kind of fatherly presence to their advisory sessions with the queen. Some also shared with the queen the kind of upbringing and social graces that made her comfortable. Compared to the queen, Margaret Thatcher certainly had a very different childhood and education. But in many ways she and Elizabeth II have perhaps more in common than the queen had with some of her previous PMs. Both women are about the same age. They are mothers and grandmothers, and most important, they share the same Victorian beliefs. Mrs. Thatcher's deeply held royalist devotion must provide an additional bond.

THE HONORABLE LADY **81**

Politically, there certainly must be differences of opinion between queen and prime minister. However, since the queen is constitutionally bound not to interfere in political matters, these differences will remain a secret between the two. Whatever the queen's feelings for Mrs. Thatcher, after meeting weekly for more than ten years, they must have found some sort of camaraderie and accommodation.

Perhaps their strongest disagreements concern their different attitudes toward the British Commonwealth, that loose arrangement that serves as a strong bond between England and its former colonies. It is the queen who provides the cement that holds this bond in place. In turn, the Commonwealth gives greater meaning to the institution of the monarchy. Margaret Thatcher has often been disdainful of the continued importance of the Commonwealth. She looks more toward maintaining relationships with the other countries of western Europe and with the United States to further Britain's interests. Any clashes between Mrs. Thatcher and the queen may have been on this point, among others.

Critics often accuse Margaret Thatcher of assuming prerogatives that belong to the Crown. She has occasionally lapsed into using the royal "we," something the queen herself rarely does. Gleeful reporters have caught the prime minister saying things like, "We have become a grandmother." That does not go over well with critics.

Nevertheless, by the end of her first term in office, Mrs. Thatcher had won the hearts of many people who, years ago, would never have supported a Tory. Her ability to carry these new supporters along through two more victories at the polls attested to her skill, her intelligence, and perhaps also to that Thatcher lucky streak.

7

THE FALKLANDS WAR

In 1982 Margaret Thatcher went to war. More precisely, she sent the British navy to war. When it was all over, she was a heroine, Britain stood a little taller, and the Conservative party won a landslide victory in 1983. But we are getting ahead of our story. At the beginning of 1982 things didn't look so bright for Mrs. Thatcher.

"I want to put the 'Great' back into Great Britain," Mrs. Thatcher had said when she first entered Downing Street. She felt that the country she loved was becoming a second-rate nation, and she worried that the qualities that had made England great would fade away into legend, like King Arthur's Camelot.

Although many British people felt the same way about their

country, few believed that Mrs. Thatcher could do better than her predecessors to restore Britain's image in the world. Nothing in her experience had prepared her to make foreign-policy decisions. True, she had stood up to the Soviet Union and to other national leaders at European Community conferences. But career diplomats and foreign office experts flinched whenever she traveled abroad on official business. They were never sure what their outspoken prime minister might say or do. Diplomatic deviousness is not part of her makeup. She speaks bluntly at home and abroad, saying exactly what she means. To Mrs. Thatcher, Britain and British interests always come first. This "Britain first" attitude is not always well received abroad.

Mrs. Thatcher, like many other Britons, remembers a time when Britain was a major naval power and the center of a mighty empire on which the sun never set. But by the time she entered Number 10 Downing Street, Great Britain was no longer the proud imperial nation of her childhood. It had become demoralized and disspirited during the political and economic upheavals of the postwar years. The days of the empire had passed. India, various African colonies, and some island colonies such as Jamaica had been granted independence after World War II. They were now linked to Britain only through the British Commonwealth. With the disappearance of its empire, Britain had lost many economic advantages, such as markets for its manufactured goods, and thousands upon thousands of colonial army and civil service jobs. More important, the mythical glory of the British Empire was gone. One of the most humiliating moments occurred in 1956 when Britain, France, and Israel waged a military action against Egypt. They hoped to restore free passage for all nations through the Suez Canal, then an important passage for ships journeying from the Mediterranean to India and other countries in Asia. Egypt had nationalized the canal in 1956. Because the rest of the world, including the United States, did not support the military move against Egypt, Great Britain and its partners were forced to retreat. After a brief period of United

Nations supervision, canal shipping and canal fees returned to Egyptian control. Although the Suez incident happened long before Mrs. Thatcher became the prime minister, the loss of the canal and the crisis it caused hung like a dark shadow over British foreign policy for years. Asserting British rights and British might around the world had become much more difficult.

Any prime minister must deal with foreign policy decisions on an almost daily basis and so did Mrs. Thatcher. She had several successes. Under her administration the long guerrilla war in Rhodesia was finally settled with compromises from both white settlers and the various black nationalist groups. "Finally, Britain is acting again, rather than reacting," Mrs. Thatcher remarked on that occasion. And, however much some of her European Community colleagues disliked her, she did manage to gain important monetary concessions for England from them.

Unlike her immediate predecessors, who fostered closer ties to the rest of Europe, Margaret Thatcher felt greater kinship to the United States. She got on particularly well with President Ronald Reagan, who shared many of her conservative views on government spending and East-West relations. However, Margaret Thatcher did not hesitate to oppose U.S. policy when she felt it was in Great Britain's interest, often to the dismay of her American friends. She was particularly angry when President Reagan ordered the invasion of the Caribbean island of Grenada in 1983 without giving Great Britain any advance warning. An independent nation since 1974, Grenada was a member of the British Commonwealth. Margaret Thatcher was embarrassed and annoyed, and she told Mr. Reagan so in no uncertain terms. Margaret Thatcher has never been one to "follow the leader." Her admiration for Mr. Reagan had its limits. A former aide reports that Margaret Thatcher, a workaholic herself, was appalled during an economic summit meeting in the United States when she heard that the President watched the movie *The Sound of Music* the night before a crucial meeting instead of reviewing his briefing books.

Foreign policy, however, was not a top priority for Mrs. Thatcher during her first years in office. All of her energies at that time were directed at achieving a speedy economic recovery for Britain. Her real battles were being fought on the home front.

It was an uphill fight from the first. Mrs. Thatcher had to battle not only opposition from the Labour party, but often mistrustful members of her own cabinet. She prevailed over her cabinet, but many of the measures she introduced were harsh, widely unpopular, and frequently misunderstood. "Maggie the Milk Snatcher" was now snatching away many of the long-established entitlements of the welfare state by making cuts in the social welfare budget. Her policies also resulted in a period of higher unemployment. As a result, there was much genuine hardship, particularly in the industrialized sections of northern England and Scotland. Thousands of workers in those areas were affected by plant and mine closings and layoffs. For the young and the unskilled, jobs were particularly hard to find, and subsisting on unemployment insurance meant living on the edge of poverty.

It is hard to explain to unemployed factory workers that it is sometimes necessary for the good of the entire economy to close unproductive factories and to reduce government subsidies to certain industries. "Why me?" those workers asked. It was a reasonable question. People who were used to cradle-to-grave social benefits found Mrs. Thatcher's strong remedies hard to swallow. So did university students whose scholarships were done away with or reduced. People were appalled that a *woman* could be so hard and uncaring and nibble away at their safety net.

These are real grievances. Mrs. Thatcher was forced to make many hard choices. Perhaps she made some too quickly and without full appreciation of the consequences. But there is little indication that she agonized greatly about the painful results of her policies.

"I want to be respected. I don't need to be loved," she told her critics.

A less determined prime minister would have caved in when faced with so much opposition. But Mrs. Thatcher remained firm, refused to make U-turns, refused to compromise. Consensus and compromise, she believed, meant an abandonment of all beliefs, principles, and values. "I am a conviction politician," she said. And she has never abandoned that stance. She has stood her ground.

Problems increased in 1980 and 1981. There were race riots in Brixton, a poverty-stricken, racially mixed section of London. There were long strikes by civil servants and railroad employees. And unemployment continued to mount. Mrs. Thatcher's popularity rating plunged. Conservatives began to wonder if she could last to the next election. But their leader seemed to thrive on controversy. The longtime outsider was determined to steer the country in the direction she had set. "I am the rebel head of an establishment government," she told guests at a Downing Street party. As prime minister, she did not feel like part of the establishment which she still criticized.

Nevertheless, her enemies were ready to pounce. And there were many enemies: labor leaders, disgruntled friends of former Prime Minister Heath, union members, civil servants, displaced members of the former ruling circles. "That woman!" they called her. All waited for her to make a fatal mistake.

WAR WITH ARGENTINA

In 1982, fate once again intervened in Margaret Thatcher's behalf. In world affairs, small unrelated events in widely separated parts of the globe can sometimes interact to produce unintended and unexpected results. Two such things happened in 1982. In England, in a continued effort to cut government expenses, a decision was made to retire the HMS *Endurance*, a survey ship stationed 8,000 miles away in the South Atlantic. The reason for the ship's position so far away from home was the Falkland Islands, clusters of land located off the southeastern coast of Argentina. The Falklands were settled by British farmers and sheepherders in the seventeenth century. Although a British crown colony since 1833, the Falklands were also claimed by Argentina. The existence of a British colony so close to the Argentinian coast had been an irritant to Argentina for almost two hundred years. For decades England and Argentina had talked about the status of the Falklands, but no decision was ever made. The few thousand British subjects on the islands did not want to live under the right-wing army dictatorship that controlled Argentina in the early 1980s. The British government was reluctant to abandon the islanders.

Aside from the colonists who lived on the islands, British presence in the Falklands was meager. In fact, except for a tiny garrison, the only British military presence in the area was the *Endurance*. The ship's twenty marines and several guns did not constitute much of a military presence. And to the budget cutters in London, it seemed a good candidate for expense reduction.

The British foreign office and the navy warned that removal of the ship would send the wrong message to Argentina. The budget cutters ignored the warnings.

Thousands of miles away in Argentina, things were changing fast. Lieutenant General Leopoldo Galtieri, the new head of the repressive Argentine junta, had serious problems. Argentina's economy was in the grip of runaway inflation. Terrorism on the part of the military government held the people in a state of fear. Dictators always look for ways to distract their people's attention from such problems. Recapturing the Falkland Islands from the British must have seemed like a popular, heroic, yet safe, diversion. Safe because it seemed unlikely that Great Britain would start a war over so tiny a territory so many miles from home. When Great Britain removed the *Endurance*, Galtieri must have felt that England did not greatly care about its few thousand subjects in the Falklands. On April 1, 1982, Argentina invaded the Falkland Islands and reclaimed them as the Malvinas, their Spanish name.

But General Galtieri had not reckoned with Britain's Iron Lady. To Mrs. Thatcher, the invasion of the Falklands came as a shock and as a major dilemma. Anything short of a forceful response would be taken as a sign of weakness, not only by Argentina but also at home. After all, hadn't all the critics worried that a female head of government would not be able to stand up to those who would take advantage of Great Britain?

What was at stake? Britain's reputation as a world power after the painful Suez defeat had to be carefully considered. Then there was the fate of the British islanders who put their trust in Britain. They could not be abandoned, although their numbers were few and the distance great. Great Britain had to prove that its resolve was strong.

To Mrs. Thatcher, there was no choice.

"Gentlemen, we have to fight," she told her cabinet, hastily summoned to a meeting on April 2. She had made her decision after long consultations with her most trusted advisers and with representatives of the military. Britain had to send out the fleet. While it made the long voyage across miles of ocean there would be time for deliberation and negotiation. But a first move had to be made. She polled her cabinet ministers one by one so that their agreement with her decision would be on record for history.

Long after the war was over, Mrs. Thatcher reminded an interviewer that the table around which the decision had been made was the same table where Prime Minister Neville Chamberlain had sat after giving in to Adolf Hitler's demand for Czechoslovakia on the eve of World War II. Her point was clearly made: never again would a British prime minister be guilty of appeasement.

Instead, Margaret Thatcher looked to the example of Winston Churchill who had so brilliantly guided Great Britain through the troubled years of World War II. Churchill had always expected strength from the British people, and Margaret Thatcher would do no less.

On April 3, the plan to send the fleet was presented to Parlia-

The Royal Marines were some of the British troops sent to the South Atlantic during the Falklands crisis in 1982. The soldiers practiced arms readiness on the deck of an aircraft carrier as they headed for war.

ment and was accepted almost unanimously by members of all parties. There was a feeling of determination, although the dangers and obstacles were clear to all.

It was a risky undertaking for the young men who were being sent to fight and also for the prime minister whose future in politics rested on her decision. In the end, whatever the outcome, the responsibility was hers. "The buck stops here," as President Harry Truman often said about himself. If the Falklands mission was a failure, Thatcher's career would certainly come to an end.

For the British public, the spectacle of the British navy sailing off to Argentina seemed somehow not quite real. Few people believed that it would actually come to a fight. The diplomats were still talking, weren't they? Just sending the fleet would show General Galtieri that Great Britain wasn't fooling this time.

Meanwhile, soldiers and sailors shipped out for the Falklands. The luxury liner *Queen Elizabeth II* had been transformed overnight into a troop carrier to shuttle British soldiers to war. And there was Prince Andrew, the queen's second son and a navy helicopter pilot, being seen off to war by his mother. It was the stuff adventure tales were made of.

The diplomats were still talking, and both the United States and the United Nations were getting into the act. Telephone wires hummed and diplomats shuttled back and forth by air as the British navy sailed ponderously across the Atlantic. Argentina seemed unconcerned. They were in possession of the Falklands. Let Britain talk and flex its muscles. They would have to deal with a supply line that stretched across the whole Atlantic Ocean while Argentina could draw on troops and supplies right at their doorstep. It would be an unequal fight.

By early May 1982, events had gained momentum. Proposals for compromise were made and rejected, mostly by Argentina. Galtieri had to cope with a restive government and an even more restive population. Any retreat on his part was politically impossible. Then, just one month after the Falklands affair had started, all peace initiatives were dealt a death blow. On May 2 an Argentine ship, the *General Belgrano*, was sunk by the British submarine *Conqueror*. Over three hundred Argentine soldiers lost their lives in the icy sea! It was never totally clear what happened. Did the submarine captain order the attack in the belief that the *Belgrano* presented a grave threat to the British fleet? Or was the sinking actually ordered by Margaret Thatcher in London? What was the *Belgrano* actually doing at the time of the sinking? Was it sailing toward or away from the British fleet? And what about the timing of the sinking? It happened just as a new third-party peace formula had been proposed and accepted by Great Britain. Did someone in the British government try to make sure that General Galtieri would reject any new compromise? All these questions were investigated and debated in Parliament long after the Falklands War was over. In the midst of the war, the world's dismay at the sinking of the *Belgrano* was soon overshadowed by the sinking of the British destroyer *Sheffield* by a French-made Argentine missile. Several other missiles hit British ships without exploding. Suddenly the entire British fleet as well as the *Queen Elizabeth II* seemed at risk. Now the war was being waged in earnest. Anxious British mothers, including the queen, came to realize that this was not just another training mission for their sons.

The fighting was fierce, with bloody battles on land as well as at sea. By the time it was all over, 131 British soldiers and sailors had died, five British ships were lost, and ten British aircraft had been shot down. Argentina lost more than 600 soldiers and sailors, three ships, and 70 war planes. Over 10,000 Argentinian soldiers were taken prisoner. For the first time, Mrs. Thatcher came face to face with the realities of war. Reports of casualties hit her hard. These were young men she had sent into battle; their death was her responsibility. Perhaps she wondered whether British honor and 2000 Falkland islanders were really worth the cost.

The men in her cabinet, those with firsthand battle experience, rallied around her, felt they needed to shield her, to explain to her about casualties and losses in war. But she did not need their urging to stand firm. While she did not hide her dismay or her tears, she never once considered retreat. When asked later if, as a woman, she didn't mind having to give orders that would lead to bloodshed, she replied, "We were thinking in terms of saving lives." Once again Margaret Thatcher displayed the mixture of decisiveness and caution that has marked her leadership style and set her apart from her predecessors.

The war forged a special bond between Margaret Thatcher and the queen. Each day the prime minister called the queen with news about the ship on which Prince Andrew was serving. This was a bond from one mother to another. Earlier in 1982, the queen had made a solicitous phone call each day to Mrs. Thatcher when

Margaret's son, Mark, was lost for several days in the Sahara Desert.

After the sinking of the *Belgrano* and the *Sheffield*, the peace initiatives were dead. British troops landed on South Georgia Island and overwhelmed the Argentinian army. Ten days later it was all over. Mrs. Thatcher told the reporters gathered in front of Number 10 Downing Street: "Rejoice, just rejoice!" The struggle to protect British rights had been won.

The lost war spelled the end of Galtieri and the other generals. Soon after the Falklands War, the junta was overthrown and a civilian government was reestablished in Argentina.

In contrast, the victorious conclusion of the Falklands War catapulted Mrs. Thatcher into the role of national heroine. Newspaper cartoons depicted her as a warrior queen personally leading her people into battle. They drew her as Britannia, the symbol of British virtue and resolve, and they dressed her in full regalia complete with helmet, armor, and spear. One sexist cartoonist drew her as a warrior queen in armor made up of various kitchen implements. Some compared her in a more critical vein to Kali, the Hindu goddess of destruction. But by and large, the media celebrated Margaret Thatcher, the Iron Lady, the courageous leader who wouldn't let Great Britain be trampled upon.

Mrs. Thatcher clearly enjoyed the moments of unabashed hero worship. She personally reviewed returning Falklands troops instead of inviting a member of the royal family to do the honor. And, in a number of trips abroad right after the war, she stressed again and again Britain's determination to honor its international obligations, particularly toward British subjects everywhere. "We have ceased to be a nation in retreat," she said. "We have instead a newfound confidence, born in the economic battles at home and tested and found true eight thousand miles away."

Riding the wave of her Falklands success, Thatcher made a surprise visit to the remote islands in January 1983. There she was granted the Freedom of the Falklands and was conducted through the battlefields.

With her popularity rating at an all-time high, Mrs. Thatcher made plans for new elections for June 1983. It was probably her easiest election race. The Opposition was badly split. She was now perceived as an asset within her party rather than a hindrance. People rallied around her. The Tories won by a landslide margin of 144 seats in Parliament.

She was running along according to the timetable she had set for herself. During her first term she had achieved many of her economic goals. Now she would take on one of her chief opponents— the monolithic British labor movement. And Margaret Thatcher could hardly wait to start.

8

MINERS
AND OTHER
FOES

A lthough she won by a landslide in 1983, Margaret Thatcher very nearly didn't survive to enjoy the victory.

Each year in October the Conservative party meets to debate and plan policy. The meeting is attended by all high-level party officials, who take the opportunity to deliver major speeches. In 1984, with the Tories in power, the Conservative party meeting included the prime minister and many members of her cabinet. On October 11, 1984, almost the entire leadership of the British government assembled at the seaside resort of Brighton, site of that year's Conservative party meeting. The prime minister and twenty-one cabinet ministers were staying at the Grand Hotel. Expecting a full day of conferences and speeches the next day, many had gone to bed early.

Mrs. Thatcher, who never goes to bed early, was still working in the living room of her suite on the second floor at 2:45 A.M.. It was her usual routine before retiring for the night. Suddenly, an enormous explosion rocked the huge hotel with all of its important guests. Windows shattered, walls collapsed, and chunks of concrete and plaster rained down from ceilings.

The stunned and frightened guests rushed out of their rooms to find a number of their colleagues gravely injured or dying. Mrs. Thatcher's bedroom had been badly damaged in the blast, but the rest of her suite was untouched. If the Thatchers had gone to bed early, both of them might have been killed. The explosion had been caused by a bomb planted by members of the Irish Republican Army, a deed they proudly claimed. Because of a slight miscalculation, the bomb had failed to hit Mrs. Thatcher's suite directly. Most of the explosion destroyed two adjoining suites, killing five officials and seriously maiming two of Margaret Thatcher's most important ministers. The wife of another minister was crippled for life. There were thirty-four injured in all.

Mrs. Thatcher was deeply shaken by the incident, but she bravely faced television cameras the next morning to deplore the violence and the cowardice of the terrorists. Clearly aware that she was the prime target of the attack, she insisted on carrying on with the conference as scheduled. Her major speech to the party received a seven-and-a-half-minute standing ovation.

The Brighton bombing was the most violent attack on members of the British government since Guy Fawkes tried to blow up Parliament on November 5, 1605. Guy Fawkes was hanged, but the Gunpowder Plot is still remembered in England every November 5 with bonfires and fireworks. Each year before the start of a new session, the cellars of the Parliament buildings are searched for bombs. Unfortunately, nobody thought of having the Grand Hotel in Brighton searched before the Conservative party meeting.

Years earlier Mrs. Thatcher had been notified just before a major speech that her close friend Airey Neave had been murdered by the

Mrs. Thatcher narrowly escaped death in 1984 when a bomb ripped through the Grand Hotel in Brighton, site of the Conservative party meeting.

IRA. On that occasion, too, she carried on, saving her tears for a private moment later on. In Brighton she agonized over the injured and the dead who had suffered because she had become the focus of IRA hatred. The IRA blamed Mrs. Thatcher for the death of a number of imprisoned IRA hunger strikers when she failed to give in to their demands. As the head of the British government, she opposes Northern Ireland's independence from British rule, something the IRA has demanded since the partition of Ireland into two separate states in the early 1920s. Days later, safe at home at Chequers, Mrs. Thatcher kept recalling the moment of the explosion, aware that she might not have survived the catastrophe.

Asked if the Brighton incident had changed her attitude toward life, Mrs. Thatcher told an interviewer: "Life is infinitely more precious to me now. When something like this happens, it alters your perspective. You're not going to be worried or complain about silly little things anymore."

The bombing generated a wave of sympathy for the prime minister and a great deal of revulsion against the IRA. Mrs. Thatcher continually pointed out that the assassination attempt was, in fact, an attempt to cripple the queen's democratically elected government. The incident hardened her already strong feelings against terrorism and strengthened her determination to refuse to negotiate with other terrorist groups in Africa and in Lebanon.

The IRA assassination attempt came in the middle of a political battle Mrs. Thatcher was fighting against an almost equally determined foe. While luck accounted for her escape from the IRA attack, she herself orchestrated her escape from possible political death with deft maneuvering and well-executed strategies.

The opponent in this case was the British labor movement. Trade unions, as they are called in England, had marked Mrs. Thatcher for all-out war and defeat during her first term in office. And Mrs. Thatcher reserved her strongest response for the trade unions. She often referred to her struggles against the unions as a fight between good and evil. She was going to fight them with a crusader's zeal.

UNION PROBLEMS

The British trade unions were strong supporters of the Labour party. In fact, the unions dominated the Labour party for most of the post–World War II period. When Labour prime ministers ran the country, trade union leaders were able to influence government decisions about prices, wages, and working conditions in Britain's nationalized industries.

Tory politicians had blamed the unions for many of Britain's economic ills long before Mrs. Thatcher came into office. But union power remained strong even under Tory leaders. The government was afraid to upset labor for fear that prolonged strikes might result and cripple the weakened economy even more. Managers of nationalized industries had their hands tied in matters of wage negotiations, improved efficiency, cost cutting, and hiring. During previous Labour administrations, many of the final decisions were made at Downing Street with suggestions from the Trade Union Council (TUC).

The British trade union movement had done many good things for British workers over the years. Wages and working conditions were improved, for example. But Mrs. Thatcher and others felt that union policies had become too political. In the view of the critics, unions exercised so much control over management decisions that British industry and its competitive place in world trade was being destroyed.

For example, trade union leaders did not seem to care if a company operated at a loss because it employed too many people at high wages, produced too little, or manufactured products no longer in demand. The unions would never accept the closing of unproductive plants or reductions in the number of factory workers, even though such measures might save jobs, companies, or even an entire industry.

Mrs. Thatcher made it clear from the very beginning of her first term that one of her aims was to limit union power. She felt that union power applied to nationalized industrial monopolies resulted in poor service at exorbitant cost to the taxpayers. A monopoly is created when a product or service is supplied by a single producer who can set high prices because there is no competition. She pointed to inefficient work practices, overemployment (sometimes called featherbedding), and restrictive employment conditions such as the all-union "closed shop," a type of company in which only union members were hired. These rules were dictated by union contracts and served to tie the hands of managers and the government alike. Mrs. Thatcher's greatest grievance concerned the powers union leaders had over strikes. Union members often had no say at all in strike decisions. Workers voted by open-voice vote rather than by secret ballot. This practice intimidated those who were against a strike. Secondary strikes were legal and frequently used: members of a different union might strike unrelated businesses in "sympathy," in order to create maximum havoc. Unions often used squads of "flying pickets" to abuse or threaten workers who did not want to go out on strike. And because unions had won legal immunity for illegal actions for which other groups would have been prosecuted and fined, there was little the government could do to enforce the laws that did exist.

Mrs. Thatcher's first targets were the closed shop, picketing practices, and the use of secondary strikes. During her first term in office, new legislation strengthened the power of individual union members against their leadership and provided for penalties imposed on unions that called illegal strikes. A law was enacted to compel unions to make strike decisions by secret ballot.

In 1984 the government went even further. It announced a new rule that made it illegal for employees at Government Communications Headquarters to belong to a union. Union disruptions of this high-security government operation were seen as a threat to national security.

All of these government rulings sounded like a declaration of war to the TUC. Limiting union power was bad enough; forbidding people to belong to a union was intolerable! And when Mrs. Thatcher began her second term in office, she knew that she would face a major battle against the powerful unions.

The union most likely to face her in this battle was the National Union of Mine Workers (NUM). It was run by Arthur Scargill, a communist who collected money for his union from the Soviet Union and from Libya. Scargill was determined to crush the Tory government and Margaret Thatcher with a miners' strike. His aims were political rather than economic. He wanted to promote more socialism in Britain with more nationalization of industry and more control of industry by labor. Because Mrs. Thatcher's policies were exactly the opposite, his efforts were directed at toppling her Conservative administration. In spite of the various employment acts so recently put in place, Scargill counted on bans on overtime work, intimidation, and strategic picketing to bring the government-run Coal Board to its knees. Once this was done, the nation's manufacturing would come to a standstill. Scargill had successfully employed these tactics against former Tory Prime Minister Edward Heath and against a supposed ally, Labour Prime Minister Callaghan. Scargill looked upon his miners as shock troops in his class warfare against the British government. To him, the end justified any means.

But in Mrs. Thatcher Scargill found a worthy opponent. She had done her planning, too. She had ordered the stockpiling of large amounts of coal at electrical plants and other essential coal-using installations. She had made the Coal Board produce excess amounts of coal before any strike was contemplated. And then she forced Arthur Scargill's hand when it suited her rather than when it suited him. She ordered the closing of a number of unproductive mines early in the spring of 1984.

Scargill called for strikes. To his surprise, his miners voted against walking out. When three separate calls did not produce a strike vote, Scargill decided to strike without polling his members.

It was an inauspicious moment for Scargill's decision. It was

The year 1984 saw labor strife in Great Britain as Mrs. Thatcher tried to break the power of the unions. Striking miners and their working colleagues often clashed in violent demonstrations.

spring, with warm weather approaching and large stockpiles of coal on hand. Many industries had converted to oil as North Sea oil became plentiful and cheap. Many miners saw their problems more clearly than their leader did; they were not eager to go out on strike. The government had offered generous benefits to workers in the mines scheduled for closing.

True to form, Scargill deployed his flying pickets. But this time the government did not hesitate to invoke its new laws. To protect workers who wanted to go to work, police squads engaged the flying pickets in violent confrontations. Night after night television news presented these incidents to the British public, showing workers in nonstriking mines being beaten by militant strikers. Unions were hit in the pocketbook with stiff fines for illegal strikes. And new rules prevented the families of illegal strikers from collecting unemployment insurance. There was a great deal of hardship in mining communities. As time went by, miners gradually began to return to work. In some important coal areas, such as Nottingham, mines never shut down at all. It was a long confrontation, but by 1985 it was all over: Thatcher had won and NUM had lost. Once again the Iron Lady had vanquished her foes.

Arthur Scargill continued to serve as the president of NUM and was reelected to this position again in 1988, but by a much smaller number of votes.

The year-long miners' strike created a great deal of bitterness in some mining communities. Mining is a traditional occupation passed on in families from generation to generation. Memories are long and strikebreakers (scabs) are often remembered and shunned for decades until they die. In 1984, miners who accepted mine-closing bonuses from the government were accused of selling out their sons' future jobs. And few could forgive Margaret Thatcher for calling the miners "the enemy within." Many of these miners remembered World War II, when their efforts had helped to win the war. A compassionate word by the prime minister about their suffering might have eased the bitterness of their defeat. After all, while Mrs. Thatcher fought for her convictions, the miners had suffered for theirs.

By and large, Margaret Thatcher was applauded for bringing the militant union leaders to heel. The public remembered the hardships imposed by unchecked union power: the piles of garbage in the streets, the unheated schools and hospitals, and three-day workweeks caused by a lack of electricity. Among Mrs. Thatcher's strongest supporters in 1983 and 1987 were working-class women, skilled workers, and many segments of the lower middle class. In terms of political preferences, the class difference between blue-collar and white-collar workers is rapidly disappearing in some segments of British society. In others, the gap is widening.

In 1985 and 1986 Mrs. Thatcher was riding the crest of her economic and political successes. In many parts of Great Britain people were much better off than they had been a few years earlier. Some of the prosperity was due to the flow of oil from the North Sea oil fields, which meant that Great Britain no longer had to import expensive oil from the Middle East. Britain's prosperity was also linked to the general prosperity being enjoyed all over Western Europe. Some of Mrs. Thatcher's harsh economic measures were finally paying off in terms of greater productivity, lower taxes, and higher incomes. And unlike the United States, where President Reagan had experimented with similar economic policies, Great Britain was living within its budget without excessive foreign borrowing and unwieldy deficits. Margaret Thatcher, the thrifty grocer's daughter, had always believed that one must live within one's budget. To her, this is as true for a country as for any individual family.

In spite of all the favorable conditions, Mrs. Thatcher's chances of winning a third term in 1987 seemed uncertain.

The political mix was changing by the mid-1980s. As the Labour party smarted under its losses and the defeat of the miners' union, an old-time political contender was returning to the ring. The returning player was the Liberal party, once the Tories' traditional opponent in Britain's 150-year-old, two-party system. (In earlier times there were no parties in the House of Commons. Members of opposing political beliefs were known as Whigs and Tories. When political parties became formalized, the Whigs became the Liberals and the Tories became known as the Conservative party. Splinter groups existed, but the two major parties ran the government.)

In the mid-1980s, a new party began to win some local elections. Known as the Social Democrats, this party attracted members defecting from both the Conservative party and Labour, and perhaps from the Liberal party, too. Eventually, the Social Democrats formed an alliance with the Liberal party to create the new Alliance party. The new party challenged MPs in constituencies all over Great Britain.

The new Alliance party presented a serious challenge to Mrs. Thatcher as the 1987 elections neared. No one was sure how many constituencies the new party might take away from the Tory party. In the end, the various factions within the Alliance party squabbled, and voter confidence was undermined. Even though the Alliance party won a respectable number of seats from both the Tories and Labour in 1987, the Conservative party prevailed again. Mrs. Thatcher's winning margin was not as great as it had been in 1983, but it was comfortable enough. For a third time she had confounded her critics and had steered her party to another victory.

Politicians can never rest on their past achievements. Every day brings new international and economic problems that can trip up unwary world leaders. Each decision a leader makes can create either new admirers or bitter enemies. Each decision can have consequences never foreseen when the matter was first discussed. So far Mrs. Thatcher has managed to walk a fine line between looming disaster and the political mine field. But she appears undaunted. She thrives on controversy and loves debate. She will have to face a lot of both before the next election in 1992 or, if she chooses, in 1991. In spite of mounting criticism of her style of leadership, her policies, and deteriorating economic conditions, she is determined to seek a fourth term in office. Right now Mrs. Thatcher feels that only she can carry on with the policies she has designed. Although she had indicated that she might step down sometime after that next reelection, this is by no means certain. She has been warned that such a promise might make her a "lame duck" and her admirers have urged her to reconsider. Nevertheless, between then and now there will be a great deal of jockeying among her parliamentary colleagues to see who will inherit the mantle of leadership.

9

ENEMIES, SCANDALS AND THATCHERISM

Some call Margaret Thatcher the woman people love to hate. And she is hated by a surprising mix of different kinds of people. Some of this dislike goes far beyond normal political differences. Mrs. Thatcher's missionarylike zeal for converting Great Britain to her economic point of view has called forth an equally fervent response from those who disagree. Strangely, some of those who claim to dislike her regularly vote for her policies at election time. Perhaps Britain's voters have accepted the fact that Nanny Thatcher is doing the right things for the country, even if her medicine is often bitter and even if they dislike the way she has achieved results. Like children who often respect a teacher they thoroughly dislike, many voters grumble about Mrs. Thatcher's tactics but admire her grudgingly.

One would think that one place above all others where she might be admired and honored would be her birthplace of Grantham, Lincolnshire. But that isn't true. So far, Grantham has not rushed to claim the prime minister as one of its honored citizens. Of half a dozen guidebooks to Grantham published in the last few years, only one mentions that Grantham is Margaret Thatcher's birthplace. Some local admirers tried to honor Mrs. Thatcher on the occasion of her tenth anniversary at Downing Street. But the Labour-dominated Grantham town council would not have it. She is certainly no friend of theirs. Margaret Thatcher, in turn, still gets misty eyed when she talks about how the council removed her father from the honorary position of alderman, which he held after retiring as mayor.

Alfred Roberts's store no longer exists, but there is a restaurant in the old building, which is decorated like an old-time grocery store. The Premier restaurant serves Chicken Margaret. "It's soft on the outside and has hazelnuts on the inside to give it hardness. Apples give it a bit of sweetness and lemon sauce gives it zest," according to the owner, who wanted to put Mrs. Thatcher's character across in his special dish. Clearly he is one of her few fans in Grantham. Many residents dislike the prime minister so much that they will not patronize the place. Some have even thrown eggs at it.

Grantham residents are not alone in expressing their exasperation with Mrs. Thatcher and her policies. Many of the landed gentry abhor her, perhaps out of snobbishness toward the grocer's daughter who made good. More likely, they dislike her because she and her supporters have eroded their natural power base in government. Members of the lesser nobility always abounded in the House of Commons and held the most influential government positions— that is, until Mrs. Thatcher began to shuffle her cabinets. Today, many cabinet positions and large numbers of seats in the Commons are held by self-made, middle-class people like Mrs. Thatcher herself. These new leaders have not grown up with the upper class's traditional sense of responsibility for the well-being of the less fortunate, which many former leaders took for granted. Some even deride such attitudes as "paternalistic." This perceived lack of concern for the well-being of others causes a great deal of resentment against Mrs. Thatcher.

Upper-class women in particular disapprove of almost everything Mrs. Thatcher does. Some have been driven to incoherence by her style of speaking and dressing, ridiculing her shopping trips to the popular mid-priced Marks and Spencer stores, for example.

Equally incensed are members of the academic and intellectual community, which includes university people, writers, artists, and musicians. They, at least, have solid ground for their hatred because of the cuts Mrs. Thatcher ordered in university budgets, student grants, and government grants to theaters and museums. They regard her as a philistine, a person opposed to intellectual and artistic pursuits, and a materialistic money grubber. More seriously, they accuse her of being racist, pointing to her restrictive immigration policies. But the feud between the intellectual and academic community and Mrs. Thatcher also hinges on ideas. Many intellectuals tend toward milder forms of socialism. They also feel deprived of influence in a government that now rarely uses the royal commissions and committees on which they used to serve. They feel uncomfortable with a government run more and more by business-oriented, middle-class managers who did not attend schools that traditionally produced Britain's ruling classes: Eton, Harrow, Oxford, and Cambridge. They are unhappy to be governed by Margaret Thatcher's people rather than by the old elite.

Mrs. Thatcher also has had her differences with the Church of England. After the Falklands War, she was offended when Robert Runcie, the Archbishop of Canterbury, included the dead of Argentina in his memorial sermon for fallen British troops. The church, in turn, has been critical of her deep cuts in welfare expenditures, chiding the prime minister for being callous toward the helpless and the needy and depriving them of a helping hand from a supportive government. In 1985, the archbishop attacked Mrs. Thatcher's emphasis on individualism and criticized the Conservative party for ignoring the collective obligations of society. But Margaret Thatcher's upbringing as well as her whole political career had been focused on weaning people away from dependence on government handouts. She was disappointed that church leaders did not see the moral value of individual effort and enterprise. Although Mrs. Thatcher has attended Church of England services since her marriage to Denis Thatcher, she still adheres to her father's sterner Methodist teachings.

A recent statement made by Mrs. Thatcher reveals her attitude toward "responsible society." It is one, she explained, "in which people do not leave it to the next person to do the job. It is one in which people help each other, where parents put their children first, friends look out for the neighbors, families for their elderly members; that is the starting point for care and support—the unsung efforts of millions of individuals, the selfless work of thousands of volunteers... caring isn't measured by what you say; it's expressed by what you do."

Mrs. Thatcher stresses individual effort and individual responsibility. She clearly thinks that she has done her share to create a responsible society by forcing people to make their own choices and by discouraging them from looking to the government to solve all their problems. Her upbringing conditioned her to believe that people can pull themselves up by their bootstraps if they just work at it hard enough. Today she still clings to this vision, finding it hard to accept the fact that some people need more help than friends, relatives, or neighbors can provide.

There is a real question whether Mrs. Thatcher's simple, old-fashioned virtues can work in a complex modern society. Unemployment seems to be an unsolvable problem in certain parts of Britain. Inner-city youths lack the training to hold any kind of

Mrs. Thatcher's strongest critics have attacked her decision to cut many social welfare programs. Senior citizens picket Number 10 Downing Street in response to cuts in pension and housing benefits.

job. In addition, certain problems are so big that they can only be solved with government intervention. Mrs. Thatcher's apparent inability to accept these facts has caused people to call her callous and uncaring.

Certain church and union leaders and Opposition party members point to the devastating effect her social policies have had on those who are least able to defend themselves. There are more poor people in Britain today than there were when Mrs. Thatcher came into office, and many of them are even poorer now. Poverty affects nearly 20 percent of the British population, and homelessness is rising. For every million new "capitalists" and homeowners, there are many thousands of newly unemployed poor.

Her running battles against the unions are ledgendary. Needless to say, Mrs. Thatcher is not loved by militant unionists. It is interesting, however, that even the Labour party has recently backed away from giving its all-out support to the unions. At the Labour party's 1989 annual meeting, party members criticized the practice of block voting by unions in party elections. The Labour party has also abandoned its opposition to nuclear defense. In some ways, Mrs. Thatcher's strong positions have actually forced the Opposition to react.

The church, the aristocracy, intellectuals, unions, and the multiethnic poor form an odd assortment of critics seemingly speaking with one voice. They see Mrs. Thatcher as callous, autocratic, insensitive, and oppressive. They complain that she has taken power away from local authorities and school districts, that she has decreased the stock of public housing, and eroded access to public health and higher education. They point to increasing unemployment and increasing poverty. They feel she is doing serious damage to civil liberties.

Her critics are not confined to Britain. Foreign government leaders, particularly those in Western Europe, have been bloodied by Margaret Thatcher's sharp tongue. She has been called the John McEnroe of politics because, like the temperamental tennis star, she sometimes lashes out at her opponents with tart remarks and decidedly undiplomatic outbursts. While British diplomats and foreign office officials cringe at her outbursts, a large part of the British public cheers her on. Like Mrs. Thatcher, many Britons care little for anything that happens on the other side of the English Channel. The Continent has often brought trouble to the inhabitants of the British Isles over the centuries. Also, many Britons prefer not to think of themselves as Europeans.

Like the prime minister, the British now have to rethink their attitude toward the rest of Europe. England lost out by being late in joining the European Community, and Mrs. Thatcher has had to work hard to overcome this handicap. In today's shrinking world, Great Britain can no longer go it alone. Now Mrs. Thatcher is intent on making Great Britain one of the leading players in the EC without giving up too much of her country's autonomy in the process. Other European leaders have found her to be a sharp and knowledgeable negotiator. She has given away little and gained a lot. Experience counts and it helps that she has outlasted so many other heads of state.

Still, she keeps shocking people. At the 1989 economic summit meeting in Paris, during France's celebration of the bicentennial of the French Revolution, she insulted the French by dismissing their revolution as a pointless bloodbath. The resulting uproar left her unchastened. Her parting gift to French President François Mitterrand was a leather-bound copy of Charles Dickens's *A Tale of Two Cities,* a graphic nineteenth-century account of revolutionary excesses. The home folks loved the gesture.

By now those who dislike her feel helpless in the face of Mrs. Thatcher's ability to survive setbacks, criticism, crises, and even scandal. Her admirers and followers are loyal and apparently still growing in numbers. At this point her cabinet is safely composed of ministers, each of whom she regards as "one of us," and so are the backbenchers in the House of Commons. She has even managed to pack the less political House of Lords by having the queen bestow peerages on many of "her" people. Several were even granted hereditary peerages, a rare privilege in recent times. (The Opposition takes comfort, however, from the fact that the Labour candidates won a major victory in the 1989 European Parliament elections. These elections are one way for voters to register displeasure with the actions of their government when there aren't any parliamentary elections at home.) Since then Labour has also won an important "safe" Tory seat in a 1990 by-election.

SIDESTEPPING SCANDALS

Mrs. Thatcher has been able to sidestep the scandals that have beset her last two administrations. One concerned the sale of a badly managed British helicopter company to foreign interests. One group of politicians, including Mrs. Thatcher, favored sale to an American company; the other favored a group of European manufacturers. It was a complicated issue with advantages and disadvantages for either deal. The scandal occurred when a highly secret report that favored the American deal was leaked from the offices at Downing Street just before a crucial vote in the Commons, a vote that went in favor of the American company. Critics asked if the prime minister had authorized the leak. If not, had she known, and when? The "Westland Affair" ruined the political careers of two of Margaret Thatcher's most able cabinet ministers, Michael Heseltine and Leon Brittan. A high-level investigation followed, and Mrs. Thatcher was officially absolved of any guilt. However, the matter has hurt Thatcher in the polls.

Secret negotiations about the proposed sale of another important company, British Leyland, to an American automobile manufacturer nearly caused another scandal. The prime minister was accused of presiding over the dismantling of British industry! Mrs. Thatcher and her cabinet prudently withdrew that proposal when it became evident that many British workers in the Midlands might lose their jobs as a result of such a sale.

The Falklands investigations also partly revolved around leaked documents. These documents raised questions about when the sinking of the Argentine ship, the *General Belgrano*, had been ordered, why, and by whom. Much of this information was made public when the contents of some confidential papers about the planning of the war were leaked. If the Falklands War had not been such a success, the questions raised might have been examined much more closely. As it was, Mrs. Thatcher was cleared of any taint of wrongdoing. But doubts have remained and questions may surface again in the future.

While some of the scandals concerned the leaking of information, other accusations against the prime minister have dealt with secrecy and censorship. She has been accused of manipulating newspapers and television news programs in an effort to suppress information harmful to her government. An uproar ensued when her government attempted to ban a book by a former high-level employee of Britain's security establishment. The book, *Spycatcher*, an autobiography by Peter Wright, exposed in detail the workings of the British secret service and certainly violated the terms of the British Official Secrets Act. Mrs. Thatcher felt that Peter Wright's revelations were unethical and unprincipled, and she ordered publication of the book stopped. She was unsuccessful because many excerpts and eventually the book itself were published abroad. She has been attacked for her attempts to reform and broaden the terms of the Official Secrets Act in the aftermath of this confrontation. Some, on the other hand, believe that she was very much in the right when she challenged this indiscreet book. Her defenders have pointed out that Mrs. Thatcher has actually expanded access to various points of view by removing many of the governmental rules and regulations from the media.

Many people criticize Mrs. Thatcher for her ruthlessness in shuffling her cabinet. She has dismissed not only ministers who have opposed her policies but also many who have been loyal supporters and mentors. Some of these decisions were announced suddenly and often without warning to the affected persons. She has sent others into "exile" by appointing them to less important or less visible cabinet posts or by having the queen bestow peerages on them, thus making them ineligible for political appointments. Her critics feel she wants to increase her own power and importance. Others admire her for sticking to her guns when she has made a decision and for removing those who stand in her way.

One colleague, Lord Whitelaw, staunchly defended the prime minister when he was interviewed by British television at the October 1989 annual conference of the Conservative party in Blackpool.

Lord Whitelaw had served for years in Margaret Thatcher's cabinet. He strongly disputed the allegations that Margaret Thatcher does not take the advice of her cabinet ministers and that her opinion cannot be changed. But the fact that cabinet ministers keep resigning and that Mrs. Thatcher needs to keep shuffling her team indicates that there are problems at Downing Street. Too often Mrs. Thatcher has used sarcasm and humiliation to keep her ministers in line.

Even her friends have wondered lately if Mrs. Thatcher's success hasn't made her incautious. Is there anyone in her government who can feel truly free to advise her about possible errors in judgment or bluntly tell her when she is wrong? Her husband Denis has long been a steadying influence on Margaret Thatcher, but he is getting older and less and less involved in political or governmental matters.

In any case, it's hard to quarrel with success. For every critic of her policies there are now also many supporters who feel that these same policies have brought new prosperity to Britain as well as renewed vigor, new pride, and greater international prestige. In short, the critics and supporters must acknowledge that Mrs. Thatcher has managed to put the "great" back into Great Britain as she had promised. That's not a bad track record for a woman who was a political outsider only a short time ago!

Finally, Mrs. Thatcher is not alone in being criticized. Every political leader in the world must face the hostility of those who hold opposing views. It is easy for people to criticize those who must make national and international decisions. It is easy for Opposition leaders to attack those who are in power. If we criticize, who is to say that our ideas would work out better in the end? Few of the problems that must be solved by political leaders have only one correct solution. There are pros and cons to be weighed for every difficult question. Sometimes it is a matter of choosing the lesser of two evils. When you are at the head of a government, each new law you propose, each policy you order implemented, will affect millions of people. Some will benefit and others may lose. The aim is to find just the right balance so that it will all work out for the greatest good. But politicians don't have private laboratories in which to concoct that perfect mix. They must take the plunge and do what they think is best. It takes courage and the willingness to be hated as well as loved. Mrs. Thatcher believes in what she is doing. Some may feel that her vision is flawed, that many of her actions are misguided. But even her enemies acknowledge that she honestly believes she is doing right. She is still her father's daughter, following the motto that one must make up one's own mind and then persuade other people to go along. But she also believes that all power is a trust, and we have to use our power wisely and well. In the end, trying to do one's best is all anyone can do. History will have to judge how well Margaret Thatcher has done.

POSTSCRIPT

This is an unfinished story. Almost every day there are stories about Mrs. Thatcher in the U.S. and British newspapers. Some voice criticisms of new policies or new cabinet changes. Some gleefully report defeats of Conservative candidates in local by-elections, hoping that this might be the beginning of a new trend. Mrs. Thatcher has, in fact, become more isolated, even among her cabinet allies due to her rigid stand on financial and diplomatic matters. New, unpopular tax laws affecting the middle classes may cost her the loyalty of some of her staunchest working-class supporters. Her caution in the face of the spectacular changes in Eastern Europe also put her at odds with other EC heads of state. Some opponents predict that her days in office are numbered. But

Mrs. Thatcher's staying power has been underestimated before, and there is a good chance that she will be at the head of Britain's government for another five-year term.

How will the future judge Margaret Thatcher? So far she has done almost everything she promised to do when she first became leader of the Conservative party, a rare accomplishment for any government leader! After some early setbacks, she turned Great Britain around politically and economically, although she now once again faces serious economic problems. She has stemmed the drift toward socialism and has done so without incurring large deficits. The British economy showed signs of improvement as overall unemployment declined and British industry regained a great deal of lost ground. Some of these gains were eroded in 1989 and 1990, however, and unemployment in Great Britain is once more on the rise.

Not all of the gains can be chalked up to Mrs. Thatcher's political skill. The discovery of North Sea oil did much to help Great Britain regain some of its economic power. Her years at Downing Street were years when the economies of other Western European nations also experienced considerable upturns. And politically there has been a general movement toward conservative policies as the failure of communism and socialism became more apparent in Eastern Europe. Perhaps some of the changes experienced in Great Britain over the past ten years or so might have occurred even without a Margaret Thatcher. But there is no question that her resolve and missionary zeal made all of it happen more efficiently and more quickly. And it was certainly her drive, consistency, and personal appeal in her dealings with foreign leaders that brought back international prestige and power to a badly weakened Britain.

The social cost has been high, however. Not all parts of Great Britain or of British society have benefited equally. While the South has prospered, the North of England, along with Scotland and Wales, has steadily grown poorer. It has been a divisive trend. And as we have seen, not everyone accepts her vision of a future

Britain. In some ways Mrs. Thatcher is a puzzle. The same woman who is reviled for being insensitive and uncaring commands incredible admiration and loyalty from those who work with and for her. She truly seems to listen to and care for those she meets face to face. It is a quality that disarms people who come in direct contact with her, and those people include many cabinet ministers who have opposed her policies and foreign leaders who have done battle with her in international forums.

For example, while she bitterly opposed former West German Chancellor Helmut Schmidt on many matters, Mrs. Thatcher pointed out to other EC colleagues that Chancellor Schmidt lived just a bus ride away from the Iron Curtain and therefore had special problems to consider in East-West relations. "One must think of other people's problems. What would I do if I were in their shoes?" she said. Some wonder why she hasn't applied such generosity to those who need her understanding back home.

On a different level, how does Margaret Thatcher stack up as a wife and mother? What will future biographers say about that? For her children it has not been easy being the prime minister's son and daughter. Like any woman executive, she has had to be something of an absentee mother, even though she tried hard to give her children "quality time." There are stories about how she sewed coats and baked pies for them during the years when she was a hardworking lawyer and an aspiring politician. Yet both of her children have felt the need to put distance between themselves and their famous mother. Her daughter Carol, after obtaining a law degree, spent several years in Australia establishing a career as a journalist on her own merits. Mrs. Thatcher's son Mark created problems by pulling his mother's rank here and there to his own advantage. He was something of a disappointment to his over-achieving mother when he refused to go to college and then didn't quite finish an accounting course either. Mrs. Thatcher wistfully remembers that her father couldn't even dream of higher education for himself and struggled to make the dream come true for her.

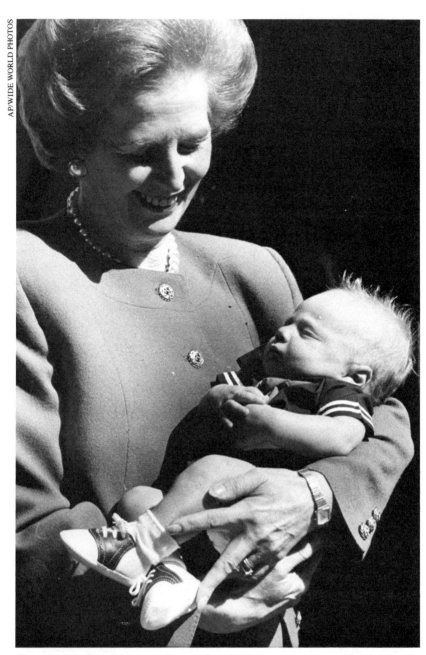

Margaret Thatcher's rich career has combined politics, marriage, and family life. The prime minister holds her first grandchild, Michael.

Mark eventually opted for distance, too. He is now a businessman in the United States, where he married a Texas oil heiress. Mark and his wife have one child, Mrs. Thatcher's first grandchild.

Not very much is known about Mrs. Thatcher's marriage because she and her husband have kept this part of their lives strictly private. People who know them have noted that Denis Thatcher is clearly devoted to his famous wife and unselfishly proud of her spectacular career. He is one of her staunchest political supporters, but he has always managed to remain tactfully in the background. In many ways he can claim a share in her political success because, without his financial, social, and moral support, she could never have advanced so rapidly. She still leans on him for support when the going is rough. No one knows if she listens to his advice. But when he can, he shields her from her enemies and perhaps sometimes from herself.

How about Margaret Thatcher the woman? Will the women's movement look upon her more kindly in the future? It's hard to know. How will they deal with a woman who has made it to the top but hasn't brought any of her "sisters" along on the way up the political ladder? How will they perceive a political leader who is proud of her "male" toughness on the political scene, but who makes sure that she is frequently seen doing "female" chores like cooking a meal for her husband or carrying a shopping basket home from the store? It's a dilemma. And it is hard to criticize a woman who surely has opened the door to high political office for women politicians of the future. No longer can it be said that a woman can't lead as capably as a man!

Then there is Margaret Thatcher the legend. Sometimes the five-foot-four-inch prime minister seems larger than life. It may be an image that has been carefully nurtured by her publicity agents, but the fact that she has accomplished so much and stayed in office so long also adds to that image of superhuman invulnerability. Mrs. Thatcher's ability to survive innumerable problems and setbacks has transformed her, too, in some people's minds into someone who is almost untouchable. Or so it may seem to her foes.

Finally there is "Thatcherism," the term applied to her collective policies and ideas. Not many political leaders have had their names attached to the sum total of their aims and achievements. (Ronald Reagan and Charles de Gaulle of France come to mind.) The term "Thatcherism" may not survive Mrs. Thatcher's incumbency at Downing Street. But then again, it might because it is a handy label for a specific set of political ideas.

And what about the legend of her humble beginnings? That, too, has been carefully nurtured by Mrs. Thatcher and her supporters. She likes to present herself as a champion of the hard-working, achieving people from whose ranks she has risen.

In fact, Margaret Thatcher was never one of the underprivileged poor. Her childhood was solidly middle-class. Yes, her parents' beginnings were humble. Her father was the son of a boot maker; her mother was the daughter of a railroad cloakroom attendant. Those two rose in the world by their own diligence and effort. Whatever deprivations Mrs. Thatcher might have suffered were due more to her father's Spartan beliefs than to financial need. As the daughter of a solid businessman, a political and church leader, a pillar of the community, Margaret Thatcher always considered herself part of the Grantham establishment. And after she left her hometown, she was always surrounded by people of privilege. In fact, her two immediate predecessors at Downing Street, Heath and Callaghan, can claim kinship with "the people" much more directly than Mrs. Thatcher can.

But the legend endures.

And what about the story of the "conviction" politician who never changes her mind, nevers makes a U-turn, never seeks consensus or compromise? That myth, too, has been disproven. On occasion Mrs. Thatcher has let herself be convinced that she was wrong, that a different approach would have been better. It happened when she became converted to the idea of "one man, one vote" during negotiations of a settlement in Rhodesia. It happened more recently when she became a sudden convert to the campaign against world pollution. It even happened in regard to England's position in the European Community. These U-turns were different from those of other politicians in that the change of heart was not a matter of expediency or a cynical ploy. Mrs. Thatcher changes her mind only after becoming a true and ardent convert to a new idea or policy. She remains consistent: she does what she thinks is right, just the way her father always taught her.

What have we learned about Margaret Thatcher? Could she have accomplished so much without stepping on the toes of entrenched politicians, union leaders, and those who benefited from the way things were? Could she, as a woman, have accomplished anything at all without appearing to be stronger, more ruthless, and more determined than any of her male predecessors?

Much of what she has accomplished can never be taken from her. She has already earned her place in history: the first woman prime minister of Great Britain and the first prime minister in this century to hold office for more than ten years. Each additional day spent at Downing Street increases that record! And she did pull Great Britain out of its long, postwar decline so that today it is once again a major player in the international arena. She has given Great Britain back its pride. Even her foes do not deny this particular fact, although they deplore her ideas and methods.

It will be interesting to watch what will happen to her reforms and to the reorganization of Britain's economic structure. Will a future Labour prime minister be able to reintroduce the cradle-to-grave benefits of a welfare state, public ownership of industry, and labor's dominance over business decisions? Will excessive taxes once again deprive individuals of a choice about how to spend their earnings? This is as unlikely to happen as it is that Mrs. Thatcher will ever totally dismantle all aspects of the welfare state. Rumor notwithstanding, social security entitlements and the national health service of Great Britain are probably safe.

Will she prevail when it comes to protecting British national interests against the growing trend toward greater cooperation with the European Community? The problem of a common European currency is a major stumbling block. She prefers to approach this matter slowly and with great caution. This insistence on caution has cost her the services of two of her most able advisers in 1989 and has led to a slip in her popularity. She seems to be confident, however, that she will once again be able to give a little while standing her ground.

For the rest, we will be able to follow Margaret Thatcher into the future, to "read" her story and Great Britain's, as history continues to unfold.

TIME LINE

1900
1914 World War I starts
1915
1918 World War I ends
1920
1925 *Margaret Roberts born*
1929 Great Depression begins
1930
1935 *Margaret Roberts admitted to Grantham School*
1939 World War II starts
1940
1941 US enters World War II
1943 *Margaret Roberts admitted to Oxford*
1945 World War II ends
1947 *Margaret Roberts graduates from Oxford*
1949 *Margaret Roberts adopted by Dartford*
1950 *Margaret Roberts loses by-election*
        Korean War starts
1951 *Margaret Roberts marries Denis Thatcher*
1953 *Carol and Mark Thatcher born*
        Korean War ends
1955
1956 *Margaret Thatcher adopted by Finchley*
1959 *Margaret Thatcher elected to Parliament*
1960
1961 *Margaret Thatcher is appointed Junior Minister of Pensions*
        Berlin Wall built
1964 *Margaret Thatcher serves in Shadow Ministry of Pensions*
1965
1966 *Margaret Thatcher serves in Shadow Ministry of Housing
        and the Treasury*
1970 *Margaret Thatcher becomes Minister of Education*

1973 Great Britain joins the EC
1974 Miners' strike in Great Britain
1975 *Margaret Thatcher elected leader of the Conservative party*
         Vietnam War ends
1979 *Margaret Thatcher becomes Prime Minister*
1980
1982 Falklands War between Great Britain and Argentina
1983 Tories win general election
1984 NUM strike in Great Britain
1985 Miners' strike ends
         Mikhail Gorbachev becomes leader of the Soviet Union
1987 Tories win general election
1989 Berlin Wall falls; Iron Curtain dissolves
1990

GLOSSARY

Alliance party   A new political party in Great Britain formed in 1983 by an alliance of the *Social Democratic party* and the *Liberal party*.

Backbenchers   Members of Parliament who do not hold positions in the government or in the *shadow government*.

Bar   The legal profession. Being admitted to the bar means being permitted to practice law. The term comes from the medieval Inns of Court in London where graduating law students were called to the wooden bar separating judges and senior court officials from the students on the other side. Being called to the bar also gave rise to the word "barrister," the British term for a lawyer who is permitted to argue cases before a high court.

Bill of Rights   A document presented by Parliament to King William III and Queen Mary in 1689. The Bill of Rights limited the powers of the monarch and reaffirmed *Parliament's* right to meet freely and often and to control taxation and legislation. This document also affirmed the right of subjects to petition the monarch. In practical terms, the power of taxation and legislation was ceded to the *House of Commons.*

Buckingham Palace   The official London residence of the British monarch.

By-election   An election held between official election days in a *constituency* to fill vacancies due to the death or resignation of a *member of Parliament.*

Cabinet   A group of *MPs* selected by the *prime minister* to head government departments and to act as advisers. The cabinet system originated in the early eighteenth century.

Canvassing   Soliciting votes and distributing election materials from door to door.

Capitalism   An economic system characterized by the private ownership of the principal means of production (capital), including land and natural resources. Under capitalism, production, consumption of goods and services, wages, and prices are determined in a free market by supply and demand.

Closed shop   A union practice that forbids the hiring of non-union workers in a particular company.

Collective bargaining   The negotiations between representatives of unions and management to determine terms for a new labor contract.

Commonwealth   The association of now independent former British colonies as voluntary partners in a relationship of economic benefit to all and with a special relationship to the monarchy. In some cases that relationship is purely symbolic today.

Communism A form of government or an economic system based on *socialism*. Under communism, the state owns all means of production and controls the production of goods and services, prices, and wages. Communist governments rigidly control all aspects of their citizens' lives, including their education, career prospects, housing, travel within and outside of their country, and standard of living. Communist states are one-party states without free elections. While in theory communism promises total equality for all citizens and total security, in practice each communist dictatorship widely differentiates between the ordinary public and the ruling elite in the way privileges and luxuries are apportioned.

Comprehensive schools Schools that offer college preparatory courses as well as general and vocational education under one roof. Most British children today attend comprehensive secondary schools.

Consensus A political viewpoint that attempts to reconcile divergent opinions into a compromise solution.

Conservative party As successor to the *Tory party* in Parliament, the Conservative party was organized in 1832 as a national organization. Prior to that date, members of Parliament with conservative leanings had long been known as Tories but on a casual, informal basis. Conservatives are still often referred to as Tories.

Constituency An area including the 60,000 voters represented by each member of Parliament. Comparable to an American congressional district.

Conviction policy Margaret Thatcher's term for resisting *consensus* at all costs and pursuing policies she believes to be right.

Council houses   Public housing provided by local councils, often in the form of row houses or small individual cottages. Also called council estates.

Council of Runnymede   Held in 1215, an alliance of tenants-in-chief, barons, and leading church dignitaries demanded redress of their grievances from King John and forced him to grant them a series of concessions set down in a charter that later became known as the *Magna Carta*.

Crown   The monarchy.

Eleven-plus exam   The exam once taken by British students at age eleven to determine if the student could advance into a college preparatory grammar school or remain in an ordinary secondary school.

European Community (EC)   An organization representing Western European countries. Formed in 1967, the organization was called the European Economic Community (EEC), but it has now enlarged its scope beyond economic concerns and is represented in a European Parliament by representatives elected in each member country. Great Britain joined in 1973. Other members include Belgium, France, Italy, Luxembourg, the Netherlands, and West Germany. Greece and Turkey have special status. Spain is in the process of being admitted.

Fascism   A form of government in which all power is centered in a single party headed by an absolute dictator. Examples of fascist governments are: Italy under Mussolini, Germany under Hitler, Spain under Franco. Fascism differs from *communism* in its approach to economic matters, generally relying on a capitalist style of organization.

Featherbedding   A practice of demanding more workers in a particular job than are needed to do the work.

Flying pickets   Pickets sent by the union to offices and factories, even those whose workers have not gone out on strike.

Free enterprise   An economic system that relies on the free interchange of labor, goods, and services to determine the level of production, prices, and wages. Most *capitalist* countries today have a modified free enterprise system under which some of these components are limited to some extent by government controls or union power.

Grammar schools   College preparatory schools supported by government and accessible to students passing a special exam. Many grammar schools have been replaced by Comprehensive Secondary Schools in recent years.

Great Depression   The period between 1929 and 1939 characterized by slow economic activity, failing banking systems, and severe unemployment and poverty in Europe and in the United States. The Great Depression affected the entire world.

House of Commons   The lower of the two houses of *Parliament* in Great Britain. Often simply called "the Commons," this house has the greatest legislative and financial powers in the British system of government. Members are elected by voters in their constituencies by party affiliation.

House of Lords   The upper house in Parliament, occupied by hereditary peers, archbishops and bishops, and life peers. Members are sometimes asked to serve in a government, and lords can delay enactment of new laws.

Inflation   A sharp increase in prices caused by an oversupply of money in circulation compared to the supply of goods and services available in the economy. During an inflationary period, the value of money decreases while the value of goods increases.

Irish Republican Army (IRA)   Originally formed to end British rule in Ireland and now devoted to ending British rule and Protestant domination in Northern Ireland, which is still part of Great Britain.

Junta A coalition of military leaders who have taken over a government and who rule without civilian controls.

Labour party One of Great Britain's two major political parties. The Labour party was first formed outside the Parliamentary system in 1893. The party briefly formed minority governments in 1924 and 1929–1932, but finally supplanted the Liberal party as the official *Opposition* party in 1945 by winning more seats in Parliament than the *Liberals.*

Liberal party One of Britain's major political parties until the *Labour party* won a greater number of Parliamentary seats. The Liberals are the successors to the *Whig party.* Until 1832, "Whig" was the name given to certain liberal MPs. A national Liberal party was officially formed in the 1860s.

Lords spiritual High Anglican church officials, usually bishops and archbishops, appointed to the *House of Lords* by the monarch on the advice of the *prime minister.*

Lords temporal Hereditary peers who have an inherited right to a seat in the *House of Lords,* and life peers who have been granted this privilege by the monarch but cannot pass on the title to the next generation.

Magna Carta A charter granted to his barons by King John in 1215 at *Runnymede,* giving England's feudal lords specific privileges and rights to protect them against royal abuse of power.

Ministers *Members of Parliament* appointed by the *prime minister* to the *cabinet* or to head various government departments.

MP *Member of Parliament* elected by voters to represent a certain constituency.

National Union of Mine Workers (NUM) A major labor union in Great Britain.

Nazism The *fascist* political and social doctrine of Adolf Hitler and his National Socialist party which controlled Germany from 1933 to 1945.

No-confidence vote   In the British *Parliament,* the party in power can be forced to call for new elections when such a vote is demanded by the Opposition leader and when many members of the ruling party vote against their own leadership. Such votes are only rarely successful.

North Atlantic Treaty Organization (NATO)   An alliance of thirteen Western European nations, Canada, and the United States, formed in 1949 for mutual protection and defense against the Soviet Union and its Warsaw Pact allies in Eastern Europe.

Number 10 Downing Street   The official residence and offices used in London by British *prime ministers.*

Opposition party   The party with the second highest number of seats in *Parliament.* The Opposition is given special question periods in Parliament to raise matters of concern and must be ready at all times to take office if asked to form a new government.

Parliament   A legislative body consisting, in Great Britain, of the elected *House of Commons,* representing the population at large, and the hereditary and appointed *House of Lords,* representing the clergy and the nobility. The word also refers to the buildings in which these two houses meet in separate chambers.

PM   The prime minister. The leader of the party winning the majority of votes in the *House of Commons* during a general election automatically becomes prime minister when asked by the monarch to form a new government. Party leaders are *members of Parliament* elected by their peers to the leadership position. The prime minister is the acting head of government with the power to appoint judges, recommend candidates for life peerages, and set legislative priorities. Prime ministers also serve as intermediaries between *Parliament* and the monarch.

Privy Council   The large group of advisers to the monarch prior the early eighteenth century. The formation of the *cabinet* system made this council obsolete, although it still exists. Today all members of the cabinet must also be members of the Privy Council. Other members, appointed for life on the advice of the *prime minister,* include eminent people from the United Kingdom and *Commonwealth* nations. The council has about four hundred members, but the full council is seldom called.

Scabs   Workers who cross picket lines during a strike or who replace striking workers during a walkout.

Secondary strike   The illegal union practice of picketing companies that do business with a striking industry or firm.

Shadow cabinet   While the ministers in the majority party (the party in power) run government departments and formulate government policy, their counterparts in the *Opposition party* keep current with what is going on and formulate their own policies so that they can, at any moment, take over running the government if their party resumes power.

Social Democratic party (SDP)   A political party formed in 1981 and made up mostly of former members of the Labour party, with some former Liberals and *Conservatives.* In 1983, the SDP joined the *Liberal party* to form the *Alliance party.*

Socialism   A political and economic theory based on public ownership of a country's natural resources and its principal means of production. The aims of socialism are to achieve a more equitable distribution of income and living conditions for all members of society. Socialism differs from *communism* in that it is basically an economic system rather than a form of government, and that it can exist within a multi-party democratic political system.

Tories   The Tories were the predecessors of today's *Conservatives*. Members of the Conservative party, particularly the most conservative wing of the party, are still often referred to as Tories.

Trade Union Council (TUC)   In Great Britain, the joint organization of trade unions, or labor unions.

Welfare state   A social system based on government's takeover of responsibility for the general welfare of citizens. In Great Britain's post–World War II period, the term was applied to the policies dealing with the widespread system of government grants to individuals and institutions.

Whigs   The Whigs were the forerunners of today's *Liberals*. The more liberal members of Parliament before the mid-nineteenth century were known as Whigs.

Wildcat strike   A strike by workers, not authorized by their union leadership.

BIBLIOGRAPHY

Cosgrave, Patrick. *Margaret Thatcher, A Tory and Her Party*. London: Hutchinson, 1978.

Farr, Diana. *Five at Ten*. New York: Oxford University Press, 1985.

Feely, Terence. *Number 10: The Private Lives of Six Prime Ministers*. London: Sidgwick & Jackson, 1982.

Fraser, Antonia. *The Warrior Queens*. New York: Knopf, 1989.

Gardiner, George. *Margaret Thatcher*. London: William Kimber, 1975.

Harris, Kenneth. *Thatcher*. Boston: Little, Brown, 1988.

Jenkins, Peter. *Mrs. Thatcher's Revolution*. Cambridge: Harvard University Press, 1988.

Junor, Penny. *Margaret Thatcher*. London: Sidgwick & Jackson, 1983.

Kavanagh, Dennis. *Thatcherism and British Politics*. New York: Oxford University Press, 1987.

Lewis, Russel. *Margaret Thatcher*. London: Routledge & Kegan Paul, 1975.

Minogue, Kenneth, and Michael Biddiss, eds. *Thatcherism, Personality and Politics*. New York: St. Martin's Press, 1987.

Young, Hugo. *The Iron Lady*. New York: Farrar, Straus & Giroux, 1989.

Many American and British magazine and newspaper articles spanning the last ten years were used in the preparation of this biography.

My thanks to Peter McInally of the British Information Office in New York for his help in providing accurate information about the British system of government.

INDEX

ABOUT
THE AUTHOR

Marietta D. Moskin has degrees from Barnard College and the University of Wisconsin. She worked as a business economist before becoming involved with children's books as a reviewer for the Child Study Association. Her reviewing led to writing, and among her titles are *Sky Dragons and Flaming Swords* and *I Am Rosemarie*. Ms. Moskin lives in New York City.